STATE SECRETS

A DOCUMENTATION OF THE SECRET REVOLUTIONARY MAINSPRING GOVERNING ANGLO-AMERICAN POLITICS

Translated from the
French edition of
COMTE LÉON DE PONCINS'
Top Secret
by
Timothy Tindal-Robertson

DEVON
BRITONS PUBLISHING COMPANY
MCMLXXV

ISBN: 978-2-925369-78-3
Printed in the USA.

CONTENTS

INTRODUCTION

When one considers the gigantic economic power and the crushing industrial superiority of the United States in the modern world, and the decadence and partial ruin of the old European states, ravaged and bled white by a series of wars and revolutions, it becomes apparent that the western world has virtually succumbed to a state of vassalage under America, and accordingly has to endure the latter's political repercussions.

Whether we like it or not, the decisions of the American Government are of absolutely vital interest to our countries, and accordingly we have every reason to study with care the turn of events in influential circles in the USA.

Now it is an established fact that some of the dramatic events in the Second World War brought to light with brutal clarity the preponderant influence which was exerted by anonymous, irresponsible and elusive occult forces on the vital decisions taken by some of the American leaders—decisions which have and will determine the future of the world—and which became particularly evident in the course of F. D. Roosevelt's virtual dictatorship.

As we have said, this conclusion is an established fact, and we will shortly produce the evidence to prove it, but meanwhile we must point out that we are not attempting to write a complete history of the inside story of American politics. This would be impossible, for it is not easy to unveil the secrecy with which the occult forces cover their actions. Our aim is much more modest. We intend to bring to light part of the evidence, in the same way that the beam of a torch abruptly pierces the darkness of night and reveals people and things which had been hidden until then. It is absolutely essential for the forces of the occult to act under cover of mist and darkness if their work is to succeed.

However, by means of irrefutable facts and documents we are in a position to prove every statement we advance, and in this manner we propose to demonstrate the action of these occult forces in the course of certain crucial periods of American and Western political history, namely :

1. The entry of the United States into the First World War (the Landman document), followed by the Treaty of Versailles.
2. The preparation of the Second World War (the Montigny-Ludwig documents).
3. The mysterious Yalta agreements (the Zabrousky document).
4. American war policy (the Morgenthau documents); the aerial war in Europe (the Lindemann document); the Nuremberg trial.
5. The Korean war; the Sorge spy ring (the MacArthur and Willoughby documents).
6. The Brownell-Truman controversy.
7. The political advisers of the White House under President Nixon.

By means of patient research I have assembled in this book a collection of documents which are not actually secret in themselves, but which have been published in different countries in varying circumstances, in partial, fragmentary, or diluted forms, so that they have remained virtually unknown to the public at large.

The Zabrousky document is unknown outside Spain; the Morgenthau documents, which have recently been published in the USA, are unknown in France; and the Willoughby, MacArthur and Flynn documents have only reached a limited public of specialists even in America.

Collected together in this study for the first time, they create a coherent impact which they do not possess individually. Nevertheless, in the course of this work I have never advanced a conclusion which does not rest upon documents of absolutely unimpeachable authority.

Thus my endeavour is to make available to my readers the awareness of the existence of certain subterranean forces which threaten to undermine the future of our ancient western civilization.

I

THE LANDMAN DOCUMENT

Is it possible, is it even conceivable that the Jews, by sheer weight of their influence alone, could unleash a world war? It is probably unbelievable, and yet this is exactly what has happened three times in the course of the last half century, in 1900, with the Transvaal war, in 1917, with the entrance of the Americans into the war on the side of the Allies, and in 1939, with the commencement of the Second World War.

In this chapter I am simply going to deal with the case of the entry of the United States into the First World War in 1917 on the side of the Allies, and I will show that this contention rests on solid proof.

Let us briefly recall the facts. By 1917 the English–French alliance was in a difficult position and in danger of losing the war against Imperial Germany. The latter, whose hands had been freed from the Russian front by the Bolshevik Revolution in 1917, was about to hurl all its strength against the western front, which was in danger of being swept away by the violence of their attack. The Allies urgently needed American aid.

The United States did not hesitate to enter the war on the Allies' side. The official pretext invoked in favour of this move was the sinking of the English liner, *Lusitania*, by a German submarine, which resulted in the deaths of a certain number of American passengers.

But the negotiations and pressures which brought about this situation are the subject of this chapter, for the facts which we are about to relate are virtually unknown to the public.

In 1929 a Polish writer, E. Malynski, published a book revealing the unknown facts behind these historic events entitled *La Démocratie victorieuse*, a work which was subsequently shown to be quite prophetic.

Basing his argument on a profound knowledge of international politics and upon a logical deduction of the facts, Malynski concluded that America's entrance into the war on the side of the Allies was due to Jewish influence.

"If there had not been the *Lusitania* affair, the asphyxiating gases, or the intrigues of German and Austrian ambassadors on American territory, in which they were surely not unique, other ways would have been found to achieve the same results. No provocation would have been too severe to obtain them, since democracy was in danger and it urgently needed American intervention to come to its aid.

"Democracy was in danger, and that is the most important point and indeed the pivot of all contemporary history. The rest is just empty meaningless phrases, fodder which is thrown to beasts who are being led to the slaughter-house.

"The apparent spontaneity of their enthusiasm for war, which shook the American people, should not astonish those who know America, or who lived there for some years before 1914. For at that time thousands and thousands of non-Jewish people, who had nevertheless been intoxicated by a costly and clever publicity campaign, demanded at the tops of their voices that diplomatic and commercial relations should be broken off with the Tsar's government—a measure which would gravely prejudice the American portfolio—for the sole reason that a mean and obscure little Jew, who was completely unknown in his own town, but whose international ubiquity had organized his defence, had been brought before a court of assize and the regular jury of a provincial city in the Russian empire on a charge, whether justly or unjustly, of committing a ritual murder.

"On both occasions, the result was exactly the same: the nation which above all others claims to be free and in sovereign command of its own destiny was brainwashed to the hilt.

"In 1914 any American would have laughed to scorn the idea that in three years time he would be struggling and suffering in France for the sake of affairs which had no connection with those of his own country.

"And yet, when 1917 came, the same man enlisted enthusiastically. Every soldier whom we happened to interview and questioned as to his personal motives for fighting, invariably replied: 'we are fighting for democracy'. They were one step ahead of their fellow soldiers from other nations, who went for their own country's sake.

"It is only when we realize that France was invaded by hundreds of thousands of inhabitants from Massachusetts, Pennsylvania, Florida, Illinois, Wyoming, California, Louisiana, and subsequently from Ontario, Manitoba, Rhodesia and New South Wales, whose only possible motive was to hasten the triumph of democracy, that we begin to understand something of the power of Israel. The power to stir up a whole nation of solid, egoistical and utilitarian individuals, and to persuade them that their greatest privilege is to set out and get themselves killed at the uttermost ends of the earth, with no hope of gain for themselves or their children and almost without their understanding against or for whom they are fighting, or why, is a simply incredible phenomenon which makes one afraid when one comes to think about it."

(E. Malynski: *La Démocratie victorieuse*)

I remember very well showing this book to the director of a big London daily paper, and asking him his opinion of it. He said that British opinion would never accept it, and he did not conceal from me the fact that he thought the author was suffering from a form of mania.

However, in March 1936, a Zionist Jew named Samuel Landman published a work called *Great Britain, The Jews and Palestine* under the auspices of the Zionist Association, which deals with Zionism and the entry of the United States into the war. As the preface of the book clearly states, the author is a very well-known English Zionist. He was the honorary secretary of the Zionist Council of the United Kingdom in 1912, editor of *The Zionist* from 1913–1914, and author of various Zionist publications which came out during the war. From 1917–1922 he was the solicitor and secretary of the Zionist organization, and later became its legal adviser. As a Jewish document, therefore, it may be considered to carry official weight.

Landman's work contains a staggering confirmation of Malynski's thesis. Needless to say, he does not reveal everything, but what he does state reveals a number of stupefying horizons, for he proves in detail that it is the Jews, set in motion, as they themselves admit, by their own exclusively Jewish interests and possessions, who launched America into the world war. The passage which follows is taken without abridgement from the opening pages of Landman's *Great Britain, The Jews and Palestine:*

"As the Balfour Declaration originated in the War Office, was consummated in the Foreign Office and is being implemented in the Colonial Office, and as some of those responsible for it have passed away or have retired since its migrations from Department to Department, there is necessarily some confusion or misunderstanding as to its *raison d'être* and importance to the parties primarily concerned. It would, therefore, seem opportune to recapitulate briefly the circumstances, the inner history and incidents that eventually led to the British Mandate for Palestine.

"Those who assisted at the birth of the Balfour Declaration were few in number. This makes it important to bring into proper relief the services of one who, owing above all to his modesty, has hitherto remained in the background. His services however should take their proper place in the front rank alongside of those Englishmen of vision whose services are more widely known, including the late Sir Mark Sykes, the Rt. Hon. W. Ormsby Gore, the Rt. Hon. Sir Ronald Graham, General Sir George Macdonagh and Mr. G. H. Fitzmaurice.

"In the early years of the War great efforts were made by the Zionist Leaders, Dr. Weizmann and Mr. Sokolow, chiefly through the late Mr. C. P. Scott of the *Manchester Guardian*, and Sir Herbert Samuel, to induce the Cabinet to espouse the cause of Zionism.

"These efforts were, however, without avail. In fact, Sir Herbert Samuel has publicly stated that he had no share in the initiation of the negotiations which led to the Balfour Declaration. (*England and Palestine*, a lecture delivered by Sir Herbert Samuel and published by the Jewish Historical Society, February 1936.) The actual initiator was Mr. James A. Malcolm and the following is a brief account of the circumstances in which the negotiations took place.

"During the critical days of 1916 and of the impending defection of Russia, Jewry, as a whole, was against the Czarist regime and had hopes that Germany, if victorious, would in certain circumstances give them Palestine. Several attempts to bring America into the War on the side of the Allies by influencing influential Jewish opinion were made and had failed. Mr. James A. Malcolm, who was already aware of German pre-war efforts to secure a foothold in Palestine through the Zionist Jews and of the abortive Anglo-French démarches at Washington and New York; and knew that Mr. Woodrow Wilson, for good and sufficient reasons, always attached the greatest possible importance to the advice of a very prominent Zionist (Mr. Justice Brandeis, of the US Supreme Court); and was in close touch with Mr. Greenberg, Editor of the *Jewish Chronicle* (London); and knew that several important Zionist Jewish leaders had already gravitated to London from the Continent on the *qui vive* awaiting events; and appreciated and realized the depth and strength of Jewish national aspirations; spontaneously took the initiative, to convince first of all Sir Mark Sykes, Under-Secretary to the War Cabinet, and afterwards M. Georges Picot, of the French Embassy in London, and M. Goût of the Quai d'Orsay (Eastern Section), that the best and perhaps the only way (which proved so to be) to induce the American President to come into the War was to secure the co-operation of Zionist Jews by promising them Palestine, and thus enlist and mobilize the hitherto unsuspectedly powerful forces of Zionist Jews in America and elsewhere in favour of the Allies on a *quid pro quo* contract basis. Thus, as will be seen, the Zionists, having carried out their part, and greatly helped to bring America in, the Balfour Declaration of 1917 was but the public confirmation of the necessarily secret 'gentleman's' agreement of 1916 made with the previous knowledge, acquiescence and/or approval of the Arabs and of the British, American, French and other Allied Governments, and not merely a voluntary altruistic and romantic gesture on the part of Great Britain as certain people either through pardonable ignorance assume or unpardonable illwill would represent or misrepresent.

"Sir Mark Sykes was Under-Secretary to the War Cabinet specially concerned with Near Eastern affairs, and, although at the time scarcely acquainted with the Zionist movement, and unaware of the existence of its leaders, he had the flair to respond to the arguments advanced by Mr. Malcolm as to the strength and importance of this movement in Jewry, in spite of the fact that many wealthy and prominent international or semi-assimilated Jews in Europe and America were openly or tacitly opposed to it (Zionist movement) or timidly indifferent. MM. Picot and Goût were likewise receptive.

"An interesting account of the negotiations carried on in London and Paris, and subsequent developments, has already appeared in the Jewish press and need not be repeated here in detail, except to recall that immediately after the 'gentleman's' agreement between Sir Mark Sykes, authorized by the War Cabinet, and the Zionist leaders, cable facilities through the War Office, the Foreign Office and British Embassies, Legations, etc., were given to the latter to communicate the glad tidings to their friends and organizations in America and elsewhere, and the change in official and public opinion as reflected in the American press in favour of joining the Allies in the War, was as gratifying as it was surprisingly rapid.

"The Balfour Declaration, in the words of Prof. H. M. V. Temperley, was a 'definite contract between the British Government and Jewry' (*History of the Peace Conference in Paris*, vol. 6, p. 173). The main consideration given by the Jewish people (represented at the time by the leaders of the Zionist Organization) was their help in bringing President Wilson to the aid of the

Allies. Moreover, officially interpreted at the time by Lord Robert Cecil as 'Judea for the Jews' in the same sense as 'Arabia for the Arabs', the Declaration sent a thrill throughout the world. The prior Sykes-Picot Treaty of 1916, according to which Northern Palestine was to be politically detached and included in Syria (French sphere), was subsequently, at the instance of the Zionist leaders, amended (by the Franco-British Convention of December 1920, Cmd. 1195) so that the Jewish National Home should comprise the whole of Palestine in accordance with the promise previously made to them for their services by the British, Allied and American Governments, and to give full effect to the Balfour Declaration, the terms of which had been settled and known to all Allied and associated belligerents, including Arabs, before they were made public.

"In Germany, the value of the bargain to the Allies, apparently, was duly and carefully noted. In his *Through Thirty Years* Mr. Wickham Steed, in a chapter appreciative of the value of Zionist support in America and elsewhere to the Allied cause, says General Ludendorff is alleged to have said after the War that: 'The Balfour Declaration was the cleverest thing done by the Allies in the way of propaganda, and that he wished Germany had thought of it first' (vol. 2, p. 392). As a matter of fact, this was said by Ludendorff to Sir Alfred Mond (afterwards Lord Melchett), soon after the War. The fact that it was Jewish help that brought USA into the War on the side of the Allies has rankled ever since in German— especially Nazi—minds, and has contributed in no small measure to the prominence which anti-Semitism occupies in the Nazi programme."

(S. Landman : *Great Britain, The Jews and Palestine*, pp. 3–6)

It should be obvious that this is a document of capital importance, and yet the press has kept absolutely silent about it, and it has remained virtually unknown.

In order fully to understand the significance and importance of this confession, let us briefly resume the facts which led to its publication.

In 1917, the Allies were in distress and desperately needed American aid, but all their efforts to bring the United States into the war on their side had failed. It was then that the English commenced secret negotiations with the American Zionists. The latter proposed a deal : "If you will promise to hand over Palestine to us if you are victorious, we will guarantee to bring America into the war on your side." If America was brought into the war, it seemed almost certain that Germany would be unable to resist the strength of the resulting coalition.

The deal was concluded, and the American Zionists fulfilled their part of the bargain, and brought the USA into the war, and by the celebrated Balfour Declaration, the British Government made Palestine into a national home for the Jews.

Up to this moment, everything seemed satisfactory. Both sides had fulfilled their engagements. However, England, in her distress, had not foreseen the consequences of this decision. The Arabs had not been consulted in the course of these negotiations, and it soon became apparent that while one party in the British Government was promising Palestine to the Jews, another branch of the same Government was promising the same land to the Arabs through the intermediary action of Lawrence of Arabia.

These two pledges were manifestly inconsistent, and if England on the one hand was obliged to accommodate the Jews, on the other she had important interests of her own in the Arab countries of the Near East. The Jews had one capital advantage. They were on the spot in both London and New York, whereas the Arabs were a long way away from the centre of action.

At first the British Government played the Jewish card to the full, and endeavoured to maintain a precarious balance between the Jews and the Arabs. At the time of the Balfour Declaration the Jews had promised that they would not infringe the rights of the Arab population, but the whole world knew that it was an impossible undertaking, and one which the Jews had no intention whatever of respecting.

Thus, to start with the British Government was in favour of establishing a Jewish community which would be built up by immigration, but confrontations with the Arabs rapidly became aggravated. Hitler's rise to power, and his anti-Jewish position, brought matters to boiling point. The British tried to calm the Jews, and cut down on the immigration of international Jews to Palestine. But how is one to reason with the Jews when they are in the grip of their messianic fervour? The influx of Jewish aliens drove the Arabs to flight from a country which they could legitimately consider as their own, since they had lived there for centuries, and they piled into refugee camps in which they have since eked out a miserable and hopeless existence. Massacres, such as at Deir Yassin, provoked a general exodus, and hundreds of thousands more fled to these camps. The Arab States, for their part, did nothing to ameliorate the condition of these unfortunate refugees, and consequently the situation became more and more explosive for the English, who

were confronted with a Jewish rebellion armed and supported by
secret organizations such as the Irgoun and the Stern gang. Palestine
was virtually in a state of war with the British.

It was under these conditions that the Anglo-American Zionists
published a threatening warning to the British Government by
means of the Landman document. Addressing the British Government as if they were speaking to an equal, they said in effect:

"You forget that you did not give us Palestine as an unsolicited
gift (Balfour Declaration). It was handed over as the result of a
secret bargain concluded between ourselves. We have scrupulously
observed our part in bringing America into the war on your side.
We call on you to fulfil your obligations in turn. You are aware
of our power in the United States; take care that you do not
attract the hostility of Israel, otherwise you will come up against
grave international difficulties."

The publication of such a serious, revealing and compromising
document was grossly imprudent, but it was also a calculated risk.
Faced with the terrible menace of Hitler, the Jews were obliged to
run risks, but on the other hand they were sure of themselves and
of their power over the press in democratic countries. The document
had to be published in order to effect the appropriate extortion from
the British Government, but it was essential that it should on no
account come to the knowledge of the general public. Consequently,
the press in the western world kept silence, and the public remained
in total ignorance of its existence. If it had been published at large,
there might well have been a violent upheaval when it was discovered
that the British and American Governments were acting under
Israel's orders. The preparation of war against Hitler would have
been singularly hindered. It is one thing to fight for the defence of
one's own country. Fighting for Israel is another, much less
inspiring prospect.

In conclusion, the Landman document demonstrates that the
Jews are capable of exerting a considerable influence over public
opinion and the American Government, and of bringing the USA
into the war. It is a clear-cut case of a well organized minority
orientating public opinion and manipulating it to its own liking.
The Zionists themselves were surprised at the ease and rapidity with
which they succeeded in overturning American opinion. It also shows
that the world-wide influence of Jewish organizations vis-à-vis
national governments is some considerable factor, since the former
were able to discuss matters on an equal level with the Government

of the British Empire, and finally conclude a deal with the latter on a reciprocal basis.

Thus the secret history of America's entry into the war in 1917 on the side of the Allies is revealed as the secret history of the creation of a Jewish national home in Palestine—and both these events, it cannot be disputed, are of the utmost importance if one is to understand the evolution of the modern world.

Finally, it is a measure of the value of the press, which is supposed to be a source of objective information, and which is so avid for sensational news, that for thirty years it has maintained a total black-out on a document of absolutely capital importance, so that not so much as a whisper alluding to its existence has been made in the numerous histories of the First World War.

Doubtless, looking back, we may have reason to thank the Jews for pushing America into the war on our side in 1917, but in 1917 it was simply fortuitous that their interests coincided with those of the Allies. Today, in 1975, it is not so reassuring to learn that America's foreign policy is in the hands of a Jewish Zionist of German extraction, Dr. Henry Kissinger, the man who was first of all President Nixon's private adviser, and who was then promoted to Secretary of State.

II

VERSAILLES TO WORLD WAR II

Jewish power, which had been exercised secretly as regards Palestine, became more visible in the course of the peace negotiations which followed the defeat of Germany.

On 28th to 30th June 1917 a great international Masonic conference was held at the headquarters of the Grand Orient in Paris—an ultra-secret meeting of absolutely vital historic significance, at which nearly every Allied and neutral lodge was represented. The object of this reunion was to lay the foundations of a Peace Treaty, to prepare the creation of a future League of Nations, and to set out the general principles governing the new society which was to emerge after the war.

A commission was formed, and as a result of its labours Brother Lebey read out a resolution comprising thirteen articles which was to become a Charter of international Masonic doctrine.

Six months later, Brother Wilson, the President of the United States, supported by Brother House and his faithful Jewish advisers, Baruch and Brandeis, set out before the whole world his famous Fourteen Points, thirteen of which were taken in their entirety from the Masonic Congress of Paris in June 1917.

This fact may be unknown to the general public, but it is nevertheless indisputably true. We will now reproduce several typical passages from this Congress, taken from the book which I devoted to the whole subject in 1936, *La Société des Nations—Super-Etat Maçonnique.*

"This war," said Brother Corneau, President of the Grand Orient of France, in his opening speech, "which was unleashed by the military autocracies, has become a formidable quarrel in which the democracies have organized themselves against the military powers".   (Léon de Poncins, op. cit., p. 71)

"The great war of 1914, which was inflicted first on France, Belgium and Russia, then on Europe, and finally upon the whole world by German aggression, has itself gradually and continually brought into definition the character of the struggle, which is revealed as one between two opposing principles: that of Democracy and of Imperialism. . . . From the violation of Belgian neutrality to the rising of the USA, and not excluding the Russian Revolution, there is not one fact which cannot be brought forward as a proof of this gigantic duel between two hostile principles."

(Brother A. Lebey, ibid., p. 76)

Incidentally, it is noteworthy that the Communist writer, H. Barbusse, wrote in *L'Humanité*, on 9th August 1914: "This is a social war which will witness a big step forward, perhaps the final one, in our cause. It is being waged against our everlasting enemies: militarism and imperialism, the sword, the book, and, I should add, the crown." (H. Barbusse: *Paroles d'un combattant*, p. 9). Not long after the war, Mr. Coolidge, President of the United States, publicly stated in a speech at Hammond in 1927: "The chief question at stake in this formidable conflict was to decide which form of government was to predominate among the great nations of the world: the autocratic form or the republican form. Victory finally remained on the side of the people."

(*Reuter*, London, 14th June 1927)

Thus the First World War, which commenced as a national war, was transformed by Freemasonry into a social war. But it was also a holy war.

"If ever there was a holy war, this is it, and we should never forget it."

(Brother Lebey, ibid., p. 89)

However, Freemasonry goes further than this, and uses victory in order to establish a new order in the world, based on the principles of the first revolution of 1789.

"It is the duty of Freemasonry at the close of the cruel drama now being played out, to make its great and humanitarian voice heard, and to guide the nations towards a general organization which will become their safeguard."

(Brother Corneau, ibid., p. 66)

Brother Meoni of Italy declared that "future humanity must be established on absolutely new foundations" (ibid., p. 110).

Freemasonry is also revealed as the instrument which created the League of Nations, and which in turn became the very objective of the whole war. The minutes of an earlier meeting, at which preparations for the Congress in June were put in hand, state:

"The object of this Congress will be to investigate the means of elaborating the Constitution of the League of Nations" (ibid., p. 65).

At the Congress itself, Brother Corneau stated :

"Freemasonry, which labours for peace, intends to study this new organism, the League of Nations. Freemasonry will be the propaganda agent of this conception of universal peace and happiness" (ibid., p. 71). In Brother Lebey's opinion, "the League of Nations is the whole object of the war. The whole world realizes that a peace which was simply an instrument of diplomacy would be incomplete and that it should represent the first step towards the League of Nations" (ibid., p. 84).

Finally, President Wilson is openly acclaimed as the agent of Freemasonry in this work. On page 117 of my work, *La Société des Nations*, I quote the resolution which the Congress addressed to him :

"This Congress sends to Mr. Wilson, President of the United States, the homage of its admiration and the tribute of its recognition of the great services he has rendered humanity; declares that it is happy to collaborate with President Wilson in this work of international justice and democratic fraternity, which is Freemasonry's own ideal; and affirms that the eternal principles of Freemasonry are completely in harmony with those proclaimed by President Wilson for the defence of civilization and the liberty of peoples. . . ."

(Motion by Brother General Peigné)

Brother Lebey's communication to the Council of the Order on December 9th 1917 effectively sums up the whole situation :

"It is a question of knowing which is right : good faith or lies, Good or Evil, Liberty or Autocracy. The present conflict is the continuation of that which began in 1789, and one of these two principles must triumph or die. The very life of the world is at stake. Can humanity live in freedom; is it worthy of it? Or is it fated to live in slavery? That is the vital question in the present catastrophe, and all the democracies have given their answer.

"There is no question of retreat or compromise. In a war in which the opposing principles are so clearly and distinctly defined, no one could hesitate as to his duty. Not to defend our country would be to surrender the Republic. Our country and our

Republic, Socialism and the spirit of Revolution, these are inseparably bound together" (ibid., p. 62).

If the Treaty of Versailles was the work of Masonry, it was also a great Jewish victory. The principal European monarchies had been overthrown. The hated Tsarist regime had been swept away, and all the members of the imperial family who were in Russia at the time had been savagely massacred. Russia had been bled white, bound hand and foot and delivered to the bolshevics whose principal leaders, apart from Lenin (who however was born of a Russian father and Jewish mother) and Stalin, were at that time Jewish.

Revolution raged throughout Europe, and without exception all the leaders were Jews.

Finally, the Jews had achieved their supreme conquest: Palestine.

As Leon Motzkine, president of the Committee of Jewish Delegations, stated in an article entitled "The Jewish minority and the League of Nations", which appeared in *Les Juifs-Témoignages de notre temps* (September 1933): "At Versailles, everything had been minutely prepared and nothing had been left to chance. That was a moment of triumph savoured in silence."

The leaders of the three big powers at Versailles, Wilson, Clemenceau and Lloyd George, were surrounded by Jewish advisers. The preponderance of Jewish influence in the course of the debates made a profound impression on certain observers, and their opinion has been summed up by the English writer, E. J. Dillon:

> "It may seem amazing to some readers, but it is nonetheless a fact that a considerable number of Delegates believed that the real influences behind the Anglo-Saxon peoples were Semitic . . . they concluded that the sequence of expedients framed and enforced in this direction were inspired by the Jews, assembled in Paris for the purpose of realizing their carefully thought-out programme, which they succeeded in having substantially executed. . . . The formula into which this policy was thrown by the members of the Conference, whose countries it affected, and who regarded it as fatal to the peace of Eastern Europe, was this: 'Henceforth the world will be governed by the Anglo-Saxon peoples who, in turn, are swayed by their Jewish elements.' "
>
> (Dr. E. J. Dillon: *The Peace Conference*, pp. 422, 423)

Such was their success that Motzkine wrote in a work glorifying the Jews: "despite appalling pogroms, which broke out first of all in Poland, and then in unheard-of proportions in the Ukraine, claiming the lives of tens of thousands of our people, the Jewish people considered the post-war period as a messianic era. In these years 1919–1920 Israel clamoured for joy in central and eastern Europe and even more so in America."

(L. Motzkine, op. cit.)

But the era of messianic triumph was not to last for long. The streak of fatalism which has dogged the Jewish people throughout their long history struck again, bringing to naught the tenacious and persevering efforts of a century past, first of all in Russia and then in Germany.

In Russia, on Lenin's death it looked as if Trotsky was his successor designate, but suddenly and most unexpectedly a man appeared in his path: Stalin. The latter had only played a minor role in the October revolution, and nobody at that time would have accorded him much chance beside the big bolshevic leaders whose names were glorified in revolutionary annals. Nevertheless the struggle shortly resolved into a duel to the death between two giants who were perfectly well aware that neither would show the other any mercy; it was a fight between Trotsky's concept of permanent revolution and Stalin's idea of socialism in one country. Trotsky, the international Jew, the demoniacal spirit of world revolution, was set against Stalin, cold, pitiless, secret, the man of steel, who had escaped six times from Siberia, the Asiatic, the terrorist of Tiflis.

Against all expectations, Stalin emerged the victor. Trotsky went into exile in Turkey, France, Norway and Mexico, where he was finally assassinated, for Stalin's implacable hatred never forgave and never forgot. With the loss of their leader, all the communist Jews of the old bolshevic guard were eliminated, and more and more restrictive measures were taken against the Jewish population, which was eliminated from positions of command and influence. Today in Soviet Russia the Jews endure an even more severe regime and have even less power than under the Tsars—a strange and fantastic twist in the nemesis of history.

This initial catastrophe was soon followed by another, which was more swift, more brutal and more serious, in Germany. Between 1918 and 1934 the Jews were politically, economically, financially and intellectually the masters of Germany, which they had led into a state of chaos and total decomposition.

But suddenly there sprang up from nowhere a totally unknown individual who was to exercise an almost hypnotic fascination on the people. It was an almost unprecedented case in history. In 1933 Hitler became Chancellor and virtually the sole master of Germany, a master whom the whole people obeyed with blind confidence.

After a series of unheard-of triumphs, he finally led Germany to an appalling disaster, a sombre and bloody "twilight of the Gods".

When Hitler became both President and Chancellor of the Reich on 19th August 1933, the Jews reacted with extraordinary rapidity:

"In late July 1933, an International Jewish Boycott Conference (*New York Times*, 7th August 1933) was held in Amsterdam to devise means of bringing Germany to terms. Samuel Untermayer of New York presided over the Conference and was elected President of the World Jewish Economic Federation. Returning to America, Mr. Untermayer described the planned Jewish move against Germany as a 'holy war . . . a war that must be waged unremittingly.' (*New York Times*, 7th August 1933). . . . The immediately feasible tactic of the 'economic boycott' was described by Mr. Untermayer as 'nothing new', for 'President Roosevelt, whose wise statesmanship and vision are the wonder of the civilized world, is invoking it in furtherance of his noble conception of the relations between capital and labour'. Mr. Untermayer gave his hearers and readers specific instructions. . . ."

(J. Beaty: *The Iron Curtain Over America*, p. 62)

As may be seen, it was a veritable declaration of war on the part of international Judaism, supported by Roosevelt's administration in America, against Germany. As from this moment the Jews of the entire world undertook a campaign without respite to stir up war against Hitler.

The German Jewish writer, Emil Ludwig, who had prudently fled to Switzerland, set himself up as a spokesman for Jewry by the publication of a work which was launched with a great deal of to-do entitled A *New Holy Alliance*, in which he urged the conclusion of a new Holy Alliance between the three great democracies of the world.

"The foundations of a new Holy Alliance are neither Christian nor royal, and neither of the three founders of the former have any share in this one, for its principles are different following the philosophy of the times . . . the influence of the United States in this alliance will be the decisive factor. Because this new alliance is first and foremost designed as a threat and a deterrent, the chief role falls to America.

(E. Ludwig: *A New Holy Alliance*, p. 94)

"Roosevelt is watching. Since he has come to power he has made five major speeches which show that the United States stands with the democracies in the struggle against the dicta-

tors. . . . All countries may join the new Holy Alliance . . . among
the Great Powers the Soviet Union will be the first (p. 101). The
national philosophy will decide whether or not a state is to be
admitted into the alliance . . . the alliance is directed against
Germany, Italy and similar states which might adopt such
principles at any moment . . . it issues its challenge in even more
forceful language than that of the dictators" (p. 104), for ". . . the
political aims of the century are: socialism as the national ex-
pedient, and the United States of Europe as the international
policy. Is it possible to reach both goals without war? . . ."
(p. 120).

It seems hardly likely, and Ludwig makes no attempt to disguise
the fact, since he concludes his appeal with the words:

"Religions, philosophies, ideals have always been formulated
and guarded by solitary thinkers. But they have always been
defended by armed men, at the peril of their lives."

(E. Ludwig, ibid., p. 123)

France's role in this campaign of provocation to war has been
admirably depicted by a former Deputy, J. Montigny, who played
an influential role in French politics, and who was closely involved
in all these events:

"As the peril increased, people gradually became aware that
there was a conspiracy to provoke a war in which up to then they
had refused to believe. . . . At the Congress of Royan, the most
diverse and opposing points of view met head on. Both militant
intellectuals and those who were traditionally loyal to peaceful
ideas were dumbfounded at Blum's volte-face, and began to discern
in him the apostle of a new war of religion. The policy of force
against Fascism was defended by his best friends, such as Zyromski,
Rosenfeld and Louis Levy, but the Deputy for Hévéder retorted
that in reality they were paying the cost of the absurd Treaty of
Versailles, which had balkanized Europe . . . why could not the
Treaty be revised. . . ?

"This was indeed to beg the question as to whether another
war would have to be fought in order at all costs to uphold the
defects of the Treaty of Versailles."

(J. Montigny: *Le Complot contre la Paix*, p. 307, Paris 1966)

Hitler, however, was preparing to invade central Europe.

"On 5th November 1937, he held a meeting of his Chiefs of
Staff and some Ministers. His plan, as noted by his aide de camp,
and which was later found by the Allies and published after the

war, was to seek the room that Germany needed for expansion in the East, the Ukraine, beginning with the annexation of Austria and Czechoslovakia. No date had yet been fixed, but everything was to be done to increase military strength (Chastenet: *Déclin de la Troisième*, p. 181, quoted by J. Montigny). The Führer also hoped that in France and Great Britain's present state of weakness, this plan could be achieved without embarking upon a war. He was not concerned about Italy, for he had laid on a magnificent reception for Mussolini in September . . . and on 6th November the Duce signed the anti-commintern pact which Germany had ratified with Japan in the previous year.

"Such was Hitler's plan for the East, and which henceforth, as the Siegfried line revealed on the ground, *comprised no further preliminary action against France*. Considering the state of military inferiority to which our country had sunk, and that we would be unlikely to conclude a rapid alliance with any Power, the delay which this plan afforded France was a gift from heaven . . . but the war party, which had decided the roles once and for all, had other ideas: in their scheme of things, France was to be in the avant-garde, supported, rather tardily, by England, and America was to be in the rear.

"In order to convince France that she had to shoulder this fearful task, she had to be deceived, and the truth was hidden from her. Political refugees from Germany and Italy were employed in this work. Heinrich Mann, for example, wrote an article in an important paper in which he stated: 'democrats who want to save civilization have no other choice: Hitler must go'."

(J. Montigny, op. cit., pp. 102–104)

Paul Reynaud, speaking in the Chamber, told the nation that not only was France strong in herself, but that the British were undertaking "a gigantic rearmament, and behind the gigantic British rearmament is another which, believe me, will be a counsel of wisdom for the dictators, and that is the colossal rearmament of the United States" (J. Montigny, op. cit., p. 104). But as if this was not enough, another argument was deployed to reassure the French. They were told that they would hardly have to fight, since Hitler would collapse of his own accord. This is what Thomas Mann actually stated in a letter published in the issue of June 19th 1937 of *Droit de vivre*, the organ of the International League against Antisemitism:

"There is no people in the world today less in a position to wage war than the Germans. They would have no allies, and furthermore, the majority of the people are in a state of revolt. After the first defeat, the struggle would turn into a civil war. No, this war is impossible. Germany cannot wage it.

"Hence," continues Montigny, "arose the conviction, which was sustained until the fatal day, of the so-called Hitler's bluff."

(J. Montigny, ibid., pp. 102–105)

"Daladier was won over to the Crusade of the democracies, but prudently considered that it would be unwise for France to step into the front rank of the firing line until she could be sure that Great Britain would be following behind her, whereas Blum, Reynaud and Mandel wanted to get the thing off the ground as soon as possible, since the Anglo-Saxons would be forced to follow suit.

"In August 1938, Bonnet, the Minister of Foreign Affairs, was entertained at Bordeaux, and at the dinner, Mandel, who was the Deputy for the department, sat next to the President of the Court of Appeal. After the meal, the magistrate went up to Bonnet and said: 'Mr. Mandel has just told me that there has got to be a war, and the sooner the better. . . .' Mr. Bonnet recalled that France was in a low state of military strength. 'I know that,' replied Mandel, 'but the democracies only prepare for war after they have declared them. Therefore we should begin them.'

"His plan was implacable but logical. He and his friends were indeed well aware that France would have a hard fight following a declaration of war, that she would lose many men, and might even be provisionally conquered. At the worst, she would be invaded, but she has an empire. Her army might have to capitulate, but the government could emigrate and continue the struggle from Africa . . . and later, after final victory, France could be resuscitated with whatever remained of the French. Such was the plan which had been thought out by Mandel, the brains behind Reynaud . . . and in 1940, supported by Lebrun, Jeanneney and Herriot, they did in fact urge the government to emigrate. This step, however, was opposed by Pétain and Weygand and parliamentary lobbies behind them.

"This plan may seem inhuman, but it was logical, whereas Daladier's view was unrealistic. There could be no compromise between Mandel's policy and the latter's."

(J. Montigny, op. cit., pp. 147–148)

Finally, in September 1939 Germany attacked Poland, whereupon England, followed by France, declared war with a criminal lack of consideration, for both countries were totally unprepared.

They were to be rudely awoken. In less than three weeks Poland had been invaded and crushed. Soviet Russia, whose alliance had been considered militarily as indispensable, did a spectacular about-turn, and signed a pact with Germany, and meanwhile it rapidly became evident that the British Army needed a long period of preparation before it would be able to make any effective intervention, and the United States obstinately refused to enter the war on the side of France.

France, in a word, found herself in a very tight spot, and her state of military unpreparedness caused profound stupefaction among her people, who had been told that their army was the best in the world. In this position, and in order to prevent public opinion, and Parliament, from considering fresh overtures for peace, "Mandel and his friends realized that they would have to 'stir up the war' at all costs, in every direction, no matter what risks were involved".

(J. Montigny, ibid., pp. 276–277)

To the general astonishment, having overrun Poland Hitler then offered to make peace, and made no demands upon the West except that he should be left free to act as he chose in the East. Daladier hesitated, but at this moment the war party, animated by Mandel, stepped in,

"and President Daladier received exhortations designed to bring him into line . . . Mandel, Reynaud and their friends stood guard over the President and brought formidable pressure to bear upon him. Provisionally they succeeded in stiffening his morale and in getting him back into line.

"Thus it was", as Montigny tells us, "that a secret brains-trust decided France's policy at a moment of supreme gravity for the nation, and imposed its will upon the President who in consequence refused to receive the offers of peace. But Daladier and Chamberlain were dreamers who might suffer a relapse, and accordingly Mandel told his friend General Spears, early in 1940, that 'the English should take command of the war, and since this role is apparently beyond Chamberlain, the sooner Churchill is in power, the better'."

(J. Montigny, op. cit., pp. 282–283)

At the same time, Mandel was working to bring about Daladier's fall and Reynaud's rise to power, as the former Minister Lémery relates:

"At the end of February or the beginning of March 1940 Maurice de Rothschild invited me out to lunch outside Paris. He told me that Mandel would call and collect me. Paul Reynaud was present, and in the afternoon we discussed the political situation. Mandel made the point, in his habitual peremptory manner, that the war was languishing, the country was becoming discouraged, and that we would have to get out of the stagnation into which Daladier had relapsed and hand over power to Reynaud. I was asked what the Senate would do were this to happen. I replied . . . that it would accept a ministry of public safety comprising only a few ministers . . . if such a ministry could command a majority in the Chamber. A few days later this conversation was continued, this time at Maurice de Rothschild's house in Paris, and Mr. Duff Cooper was there. Again the conversation turned to the question of replacing Daladier with Reynaud, and of entering into a pact with the London government in order to affirm their joint determination to pursue the war to total victory.

"These two factors sought by Mandel were soon to be accomplished both in Paris and in London.

(J. Montigny, op. cit., pp. 283-284)

"In Paris, Reynaud was elected Prime Minister by a majority vote! Several weeks later, in the middle of June, the Allied armies had been pierced at Sedan, cut through at Abbeville, surrounded at Lille and Dunkirk and defeated in Artois and Picardy. Their front had been broken in Champagne, the armies in Lorraine and Alsace, and the Maginot line, could no longer escape being encircled, the public administration left Paris, and three million French, Dutch and Belgian refugees had flooded out onto our roads, holding up military convoys. Suddenly stripped of her defences, France fell into anarchy. At the meeting of the ministers outside Tours, General in Chief Weygand, supported by Marshal Pétain, declared that the army should choose between capitulation and an armistice, and that since the former course was contrary to honour and forbidden by the military code, conditions for an eventual armistice should be demanded from the enemy, provided that it was understood that they would only be accepted if they were honourable and would safeguard the freedom of our fleet and of our possessions overseas. The Council of Ministers were overwhelmed at being put on notice that they should study the conditions for an armistice, for the Franco-British agreement forbade separate armistices. This meant that the situation would have to be laid before Churchill, in order to obtain his assent in the eventuality of such an armistice. The Council decided to invite the British Prime Minister to attend a conference with them on the following day, and the President of the Council was charged with transmitting this invitation. As he explained at the trial of Marshal Pétain, Paul Reynaud decided to see Churchill first of all alone, and not to tell him about the Council's invitation. He would only bring him to the conference when he had assured himself of his refusal.

"However, on the following day, Churchill, aware of the insufficient British contribution to the defence of France, and stirred by the situation of our country, withdrew all opposition, and after consulting with the ministers who had accompanied him, soon confirmed that he was well disposed towards this proposal.

(J. Montigny, op. cit., pp. 284–285)

"The separate armistice became the least disastrous course for France to adopt, but it was contrary to the plans for the Crusade; furthermore, it would deprive the conspiring war party in France of the dramatic departure they envisaged, with a well orchestrated heroes' farewell upon embarkation for overseas. For if they were to remain in France, they would have to take action, and if they fled privately, their political careers would be compromised.

"The counter-attack rapidly developed. First of all, Churchill was allowed to leave without being told that the Council of Ministers were awaiting him, and subsequently the Council was informed that the Prime Minister had refused to agree to a separate armistice. Finally, a well-trusted messenger was sent to London to inform him of the falsehood, and to ask him to retract his previous consent, which had been kept secret.

"It was General de Gaulle, Reynaud's confidant, who was chosen to accomplish this mission. Towards the end of the afternoon, the Council of Ministers, deceived by their President's false report, decided to postpone the demand for an armistice. Mandel was happy, and told General Spears how the Council had been tricked . . . At Bordeaux, Reynaud resigned, and the former Minister of the Interior set out for Morocco on the steamer *Massilia*. During the trip he learnt with surprise that the armistice had been signed. He told his friends that when he arrived at Morocco he would try and set up a government in order to continue the war in North Africa with the French Fleet. As soon as he had disembarked he went to the British Embassy where, following a conversation, Churchill was notified of the situation, immediately summoned a Cabinet meeting, and decided to send out a Minister and a top

military authority to Casablanca at once with instructions to help
Mandel in his rebellion. But the wheel of fortune had turned.
General Noguès, who was resident in Morocco, and who was
Commander in Chief of North Africa, decided to remain faithful
to Marshal Pétain, put Mandel back on the *Massilia*, and dis-
missed Churchill's envoys.

"The latter event proves Mandel's pre-eminent position in the
conspiracy.

"A year earlier Chamberlain had remarked that war is not a
speculation with money, but with human beings, and it is impossible to calculate the disasters that would result from a conflict. Since then he has been overwhelmed by the warlike
declarations which have assailed him from all sides, and he
resigned himself to the war from the day when ideological
passions managed to silence the voice of reason. . . .

"Daladier was in tow, and these were his thoughts, as he con-
fessed to a parliamentary commission of enquiry: 'The French
government threw itself into the war in desperation, thinking of
the ruin that would be caused. It was convinced that France would
only be at the avant-garde of a coalition army, that the war
would last a long time, and that catastrophe would follow
catastrophe' and he ended with William II's cry: 'I didn't want
it.' He did not want it, but he did it, and he did it because he was
manœuvred by the crusaders. He often telephoned Roosevelt from
the United States Embassy in Paris, and we have very weighty
evidence as to the President's disposition at this time from the
person of Mr. Joseph Kennedy, the father of the late President
Kennedy. At that time Joseph Kennedy was Roosevelt's Ambassador in Great Britain and on friendly terms with the President,
and in 1945 he held a conversation with Mr. Forrestal, then a
member of the American government, which was so serious that
the latter wrote it down in his Diary when he returned to his
house. This Diary was published after the war, and here is the
passage in question :

'27th December 1945

'Played golf today with Joseph Kennedy . . . Kennedy's view
was that Hitler would have fought Russia without any later conflict with England if it had not been for Bullitt's (Ambassador to
France) urging on Roosevelt in the summer of 1939 that the
Germans must be faced down about Poland; neither the French nor
the British would have made Poland a case of war if it had not
been for the constant needling from Washington. Bullitt, he said,
kept telling Roosevelt that the Germans wouldn't fight, Kennedy

that they would, and that they would overrun Europe. Chamberlain, he says, stated that America and the world Jews had forced England into the war. In his telephone conversation with Roosevelt in the summer of 1939 the President kept telling him to put some iron up Chamberlain's backside.' "

(*The Forrestal Diaries*, 1952, pp. 128–129)

"Chamberlain's opinion on the importance of Jewish pressure being brought to bear in favour of the war in the United States is confirmed by a report from Count Potocki, Polish Ambassador in Washington, who warned his government in 1939 of the campaign that was being organized in response to recent anti-semitic excesses of the nazis, a campaign in which various Jewish intellectuals took part, such as Bernard Baruch, Frankfurter, a Justice of the Supreme Court, Morgenthau, Secretary of the Treasury, and others who were linked to Roosevelt by ties of personal friendship. This group of men, who held some of the highest posts in the American government, was very closely connected to International Jewry. Will Count Potocki be accused of antisemitism? The Jewish writer, Emmanuel Berl, wrote before the Munich crisis : 'All the Jews in politics hope for war and are urging towards it. Daily proof of this attitude is to be found in the corridors of the Chamber, not to mention Blum and Mandel's example. The Jewish community, as a political unit, has been and still is the life and soul of the war party'.

"This indeed is one of the truths of that time, but that is not to implicate the majority of the Jews, but only a well-organized international minority whose power lay in their wealth, their determination and in the key positions which they held in the democratic world.

"There is also another point of view to consider : the war leaders and statesmen of St. Petersburg, Vienna, Berlin and Paris who in 1914 yielded, with varying degrees of responsibility, to the temptation to hold a trial of strength—they had an excuse. They all believed that it would be a short war, and in fact no other alternative was even admitted.

"Hitler had the same hope in 1939. Stalin, on the other hand, was gambling on a long war of attrition which the leaders of the democracies and their military experts knew was inevitable. This is confirmed by Ambassador Bullitt's proposals to Count Potocki in November 1938, which were reported to the Polish government in the following terms :

'According to the information which the military experts had supplied to Bullitt at the time of the crisis in the autumn of 1938, a war would last at least six years and would end with a complete disaster for Europe. There was no doubt whatever that in the end Soviet Russia would profit by it all.'

(Polish documents on the origin of the war)

"The United States was to benefit by it as well. It would be a mistake to imagine that Roosevelt was simply an idealist. Certain remarks he made to his son Elliot reveal that he was capable of realistic egoism. In the summer of 1941, some months before Pearl Harbour, Roosevelt, who had been re-elected in 1940, still refused Churchill's plea that he should enter the war. He explained his tactics to his son by drawing a comparison with a game of football: 'For the moment', he said, 'we are the reserve players sitting it out on the bench, and it is the Russians who have the field. . . . Our role is to follow the game, and before our markers (England and Russia) get tired, to join in for the final trial. *In this way we will come to the struggle all fresh. . . .*'

"Thus, in contrast to the French leaders, who were so eager to throw their country into the fight at the very start, Roosevelt, in the same way that Stalin had, sought to intervene in the war as late as possible, when all the others would be exhausted. At the same time, he did not hide from Churchill the prizes on which his eyes were fixed: the abolition of imperial tariffs, and a general move towards decolonization, which he hoped would greatly enrich his own country commercially. Thus in 1942, at the Casablanca Conference, he held out to the Sultan of Morocco, who took it, the bait of independence . . . matched by future economic relations between the two countries.

(J. Montigny, op. cit., pp. 289–290)

"Be that as it may, France, who declared war for fear of having it forced upon her one day, carried it on for fear she should have to recommence it, and thus courted disaster for fear of a future defeat."

(J. Montigny: *Le Complot contre la Paix*)

Incidentally, a staggering fact emerges from Montigny's book, as the following episode relates:

"At this period, de Monzie, the Minister of Public Works, made a short trip to London, and all his time was taken up with conferences with his opposite number in England. A few days after he had returned, he received a pressing invitation to dine with one of the London clan of the Rothschilds. During the dessert, this lady said to him:

" 'I believe that you have just returned from London, Minister?

" 'Yes', he replied.

" 'Do you realize that you have been regrettably neglectful? You are aware of the importance of the head of our family there, and you never went to see him.'

" 'I am sorry that I was unable to do so, but I was too busy during my short stay.'

" 'And yet Mr. Paul Reynaud, who is just as busy as you are when he is in London, never fails to make this visit.'

" 'I had been invited to be given this lesson', de Monzie concluded, 'and thereafter I had no more illusions: Daladier's heir presumptive had already been chosen, and in due course Lebrun would be notified.' "

(J. Montigny, op. cit., p. 227)

In other words, at the height of the war, the London Rothschilds were able to decide the choice of the French Prime Minister. Such an incredible piece of information goes without comment.

Three years earlier, Montigny had admirably depicted the atmosphere of a war of religion which was to impregnate the Second World War, in a speech at the Chamber on July 31st 1936:

"Our foreign policy", he stated, "has succeeded in creating two opposing power blocs in Europe. The serious thing is that these two blocs not merely represent political and economic combinations; more and more it is emerging that the struggle is between political doctrines, social systems and philosophical conceptions, and their mutual antagonism has only been increased by the case of Ethiopia, the Spanish and French elections, and the Spanish civil war.

"The conflict, which rises with ever-increasing passion, is between ideas of collective security and bilateral agreements, racism and internationalism, Hitlerism and communism, and finally, between Fascism and democracy.

"From this point of view, the situation in Europe is worse than in 1913, because it is no longer a case, as it was then, simply of opposing blocs; we are confronted with self-excommunicating ideas. The other side is not merely regarded as a rival or an adversary; he is a heretic whose criminal faith should be destroyed. Europe is permeated with the atmosphere of a war of religion, which is engendering the spirit of a crusade.

"How else is one to explain certain sudden changes which have come about? Those circles which formerly most ardently sought peace, today unhesitatingly demand a war effort and human sacrifice as soon as it is a question of supporting what in their eyes is a holy cause, be it yesterday against Italian Fascism, or today against Spanish Fascism, or tomorrow against the Hitlerian heresy. The moment that it is allowed to become patriotic, the most antimilitary party immediately exalts the army with unprecedented fervour.

"That is where Europe has got to, after two centuries of struggle towards reason and progress, and the tragedy is that this progress has placed an unlimited power of massacre at the service of passions which belong to the middle ages."

(J. Montigny: *Le Complot contre la Paix*, p. 307)

III

TERROR BOMBING AND THE DESTRUCTION
OF DRESDEN

When the Nuremberg Trials opened, the whole world expected
that the German bombing of defenceless towns would be one of the
main arguments in the case for the prosecution. However, to the
general surprise, the question was not even raised.

In the opinion of every western country, the matter was quite
clear-cut, and any discussion was ruled out. The Germans had commenced a campaign of terror bombing directed against defenceless
towns and civilian populations which could in no way be classified
as military objectives: Rotterdam, London, Coventry, etc. Sow the
wind and you will reap a tempest. As the Anglo-Saxons progressively
got control of the sky, the terrifying weapon of aerial bombardment
rebounded against the Germans, and all their big towns were reduced
to ashes, in an apocalyptic outburst of bloodshed.

But there was no doubt in anyone's mind that the initial responsibility for this crime lay with the Germans, and that they
should have had to answer for it at the trial of the war criminals
at Nuremberg. Why, in that case, was the whole matter passed
over in silence?

Today we can at last produce the stupefying answer to that
question. It is one of the biggest and most strictly kept secrets of
the war, which the British and American Governments have success-
fully guarded behind a total blackout for over twenty years. Briefly,
the accepted version which was put out by the Allied propaganda
organs is completely false, and the British Government has coldly
and shamelessly told a lie.

This is not to say that we intend to absolve Hitler's Government
of all responsibility in the conduct of the aerial war, for it is certain
that had he been able, Hitler would not have hesitated to destroy
the English towns, but it is also true that the Anglo-Saxons have not
got a clean conscience in the matter.

Let us briefly resume the sequence of events which led to the
appalling catastrophe of the terror bombardments in the Second
World War, starting at 1923. At this period, the Air Force in

Britain was already developing as a separate service, contrary to France and Germany. When the question of rearmament arose, the discussion turned to the use that would be made of aviation in wartime, and consequently, the type of aircraft that would be required. Two theories were under consideration. Officers of the classic military school of thought held that the aircraft was a long-range strike weapon whose role lay in attacking the enemy army. But Air Marshal Trenchard, who was not handicapped by antique military traditions nor by moral scruples, held that aircraft could be put to more efficient and deadly use by deliberately attacking industrial centres and urban agglomerations, which were less difficult to reach and less dangerous targets. He held that its role should be to pursue the destruction of the enemy nation, whereas the Army maintained that it should pursue the destruction of the enemy army.

Such concepts, briefly, heralded a return to the days of Gengis Khan and Attila, and genocide again became an official object of war.

In 1934 England began a massive rearmament programme, the main effort of which was concentrated on the aviation industry. Trenchard's ideas prevailed and England began the construction of an armada of heavy, long-range bombers for the purposes of what was called "strategic bombing". In other words, instead of building machines such as the German stukas—dive-bombers whose role was to attack precise military objects, such as tanks—the English were building machines with a heavy pay-load designed to throw a carpet of bombs over vast areas of towns and industrial centres, and which were later imitated by the American flying fortresses.

Aerial bombing went through three successive phases during the Second World War. Firstly, between 3rd September 1939 and 11th May 1940 the air forces of the two sides adhered to the conventional regulations of war adopted by civilized countries, and only bombed military objectives. But on 11th May 1940, the day after the German offensive was unleashed on the western front, the British Government adopted a new definition as to what constituted military objectives. Until that time, any building or enterprise contributing directly or indirectly to the war effort had been considered as a military objective. But on that day, for the first time, a squadron of eighteen British bombers undertook a raid in the interior of Germany against a railway station and part of a town which were not strictly speaking military objectives. It was obvious that such a definition permitted the virtually unlimited extension of bombing, since every town and village contains buildings which indirectly can be made to serve the war effort.

For four months the High Command directed more and more violent and extensive so-called "strategic" bombings against Germany. Then on 16th December 1940 a squadron of one hundred and thirty-four heavy bombers conducted what was described as the first "strategic" bombing against the town-centre of Mannheim, without any pretence that this was striking at some military objective. At this time Britain did not have sufficient heavy bombers to make these attacks really effective. What, then, was their purpose? There was, it is true, an accessory reason. They served to train the crews and perfect techniques in preparation for the later, massive raids. But the real reason is so incredible, and so fantastic that I would not dare to assert it if it had not already been officially made public by the British Government.

In April 1961 there appeared a small work under a seemingly abstract title, *Science and Government*. The author, Sir Charles Snow, is a scientist and a writer, and in one simple paragraph he revealed for the first time a truth of absolutely capital importance.

"Early in 1942 . . . he (Lindemann) produced a Cabinet paper on the strategic bombing of Germany . . . it described in quantitative terms the effect on Germany of a British bombing offensive in the next eighteen months (approximately March 1942–September 1943). The paper laid down a strategic policy. The bombing must be directed essentially against German working-class houses. Middle-class houses have too much space round them, and so are bound to waste bombs; factories and 'military objectives' had long since been forgotten, except in official bulletins, since they were much too difficult to find and hit. The paper claimed that—given a total concentration of effort on the production and use of bombing aircraft—it would be possible, in all the larger towns of Germany (that is, those with more than 50,000 inhabitants) to destroy 50 per cent of all houses."

(Sir Charles Snow: *Science and Government*, pp. 47–48)

"The Air Ministry fell in behind the Lindemann paper. The minority view was not only defeated, but squashed. The atmosphere . . . had just the perceptible smell of a witch hunt (p. 50) . . . Churchill and Lindemann really did work together on all scientific decisions and on a good many others, as one mind. In his early days as grey eminence to the Prime Minister, Lindemann made it obvious, by holding his interviews in 10 Downing Street, or by threatening Churchill's intervention. Very soon this was not necessary. Bold men protested to Churchill about Lindemann's influence, and were shown out of the room. Before long everyone in official England knew that the friendship was unbreakable, and that Lindemann held real power."

(Sir C. Snow, ibid., p. 64)

This brief revelation created a feeling of profound stupor in England. On several occasions important people had questioned the government as to whether the RAF was terror-bombing the civilian population of Germany, and on each occasion the Secretary for Air, Sir Archibald Sinclair, had replied that it had never issued such orders, and that the bombing raids were directed exclusively against military objectives. Naturally, there had been an inevitable number of civilian losses during the course of these operations.

When Snow's book appeared in 1961, the British public expected an immediate and forthright contradiction from the government, but no such denial was forthcoming. However, six months later the truth was finally revealed in an official publication, *The Strategic Air Offensive against Germany*, published by HMSO, which contains the most exact details of the history of the Allied bombing campaign against Germany during the Second World War.

In his book, *Advance to Barbarism* (p. 184), F. J. P. Veale states:

"In passing it may be observed that the question which air offensive was a reprisal for which had now long ceased to be a subject for dispute. As early as 1953 HM Stationery Office published the first volume of a work *The Royal Air Force, 1939–1945* entitled *The Fight at Odds*, a book described as 'officially commissioned and based throughout on official documents which had been read and approved by the Air Ministry Historical Branch.' The author, Mr. Dennis Richards, states plainly that the destruction of oil plants and factories was only a secondary purpose of the British air attacks on Germany which began in May 1940. The primary purpose of these raids was to goad the Germans into undertaking reprisal raids of a similar character on England. Such raids would arouse intense indignation in Britain against Germany and so create a war psychosis without which it is impossible to carry on a modern war. Mr. Dennis Richards writes (p. 122): 'The attack on the Ruhr, in other words, was an informal invitation to the Luftwaffe to bomb London.' "

It could not have been phrased more clearly, or more cynically, and this machiavellian trap functioned to perfection.

In March 1942 the fatal decision was taken to adopt the Lindemann plan, and this step marked the beginning of the third and final phase in the bombing strategy of the Allies. It was to weigh heavily on the future of the war, and of the whole world in general.

Once the principle of terror-bombing was accepted, it was earnestly pursued as a war policy and carried out with increasing intensity up to 1944 and the opening weeks of 1945. As a result, there took place the appalling bombardments of Hamburg (27–28th July 1943), Lübeck and Cologne, culminating in a nightmare of apocalyptic proportions, the bombing of Dresden on 13th February 1945.

The bombing of Dresden is a date that will never die in the annals of history, for in sheer horror it surpasses the destruction of either Hamburg, Hiroshima or Tokyo.

It was one of the most atrocious crimes of the Second World War, and yet even as an act it served absolutely no purpose whatever.

Dresden, the capital of Saxony, was a famous town, rich in artistic and architectural treasures of every description. Normally, it had a population of some 600,000 inhabitants, but in February 1945 the Soviet armies were spreading out far and wide across eastern Prussia, Silesia and Roumania, leaving in their wake a trail of violations and atrocities worthy of the hordes of Attila and Gengis Khan. Dresden was surrounded with refugees, the vast majority of whom were women and children, who were fleeing from the horrors of the Russian invasion. There were more than half a million in the town, and it was at this precise moment that the Anglo-American High Command chose to hit Dresden with perhaps the heaviest bombardment of the whole war. The raid had no military object at all, except perhaps to show the Russians that the Allies were going to do everything in their power to help them.

On the night of 13th and 14th February 1945, 1,400 English bombers attacked the town in continuous waves, dropping 650,000 incendiary bombs, alternating with hundreds of huge explosive bombs, and the following morning 1,350 American Liberator flying fortresses returned to the attack to find the city a prey to a terrifying new phenomenon—Dresden was a fire-storm, and winds of several hundred miles an hour swept up the flames so high that they threatened the bombers and could be seen over 200 miles away.

On the following night, the Lancasters took off again for the neighbouring town of Chemnitz.

"This time", says David Irving, in his *Destruction of Dresden* (p. 155), "less attempt was made to veil the real nature of the target city. Curiously, although Chemnitz as a city possessed many obviously military and legitimate targets—the tank works, the large textile and uniform-making factories, and one of the largest locomotive repair depots in the Reich, in at least two widely separated squadrons of two Bomber Groups an almost identical wording of the briefing was used by the Intelligence officers. Thus No. 1 Group crews were informed:

Tonight your target is to be Chemnitz. We are going there to attack the refugees who are gathering there, especially after last night's attack on Dresden.

No. 3 Group crews were briefed:

Chemnitz is a town some thirty miles west of Dresden, and a much smaller target. Your reasons for going there tonight are to finish off any refugees who may have escaped from Dresden. You'll be carrying the same bombloads, and if tonight's attack is as successful as the last, you will not be paying any more visits to the Russian front."

Further on, Irving writes:

"The ferocity of the USSAF daylight raid of 14th February had finally brought the people to their knees. The sky had been overcast and the bombs dropped by the Flying Fortresses were widely scattered.

"But it was not the bombs which finally demoralized the people: compared with the night's bombardment by two- and four-ton 'blockbusters', the American 500-pound General Purpose bombs must have seemed very tame; it was the Mustang fighters, which suddenly appeared low over the city, firing on everything that moved, and machine-gunning the columns of lorries heading for the city. One section of the Mustangs concentrated on the river banks, where masses of bombed-out people had gathered. Another section attacked targets in the Grosser Garten area.

"Civilian reaction to these fighter-strafing attacks, which were apparently designed to complete the task outlined in the air commanders' Directives as 'causing confusion in the civilian evacuation from the East', was immediate and universal; they realized that they were absolutely helpless . . . British prisoners who had been released from their burning camps were among those to suffer the discomfort of machine-gunning attacks on the river banks and have confirmed the shattering effect on morale. Where-ever columns of tramping people were marching in or out of the city they were pounced on by the fighters, and machine-gunned or raked with cannon fire. It is certain that many casualties were caused by this low-level strafing of the city, which later became a permanent feature of American attacks."

(D. Irving, op cit., pp. 180–181)

Three-quarters of a million incendiary bombs were dropped on Chemnitz, but the sky was very clouded and the town was defended by anti-aircraft installations, unlike Dresden, and accordingly the results were less spectacular and less frightful.

The general attack had lasted for thirty-six hours without ceasing, and the massacre had been horrifying. The town had been choked with refugees, but the heat was so great that most of the bodies and even the buildings had been liquefied. It is impossible to estimate the number of dead with precision, but it is somewhere between one hundred and twenty and two hundred thousand. The figure of one hundred and thirty-five thousand would seem nearest to the truth. It was the greatest single massacre in all European history, and on this level at least, the Lindemann plan had proved its efficiency, although, as we shall see, it was a failure in every other aspect. The area of total destruction covered three thousand acres. The fires lasted for a week. Police and troops cordoned off the town centre and any-one seen pillaging was shot on sight. What remained of the corpses was piled up on immense pyres hastily constructed out of burnt beams, and these pyres burnt unceasingly for weeks. The photo-graphs which were subsequently published bear witness to a horror which is almost beyond endurance.

On February 16th, however, SHAEF published a triumphant communiqué. On that day, as David Irving tells us:

". . . the air commanders entrusted an RAF Air Commodore seconded to SHAEF as ACS2 (Intelligence) officer, to address a press conference . . . On air activities generally, with particular reference to those of the enemy. . . .

"According to the American Official History, the new Allied plan that he outlined was to 'bomb large population centres and then to attempt to prevent relief supplies from reaching and refugees from leaving them—all part of a programme to bring about the collapse of the German economy.'

"In the course of a reply to a question put to him by one correspondent, the Air Commodore recalls having apparently referred to German allegations of 'terror-raids'—he was currently engaged in Intelligence on German operations—and, once spoken, the word remained in the mind of the correspondent of the Associated Press. Within an hour, the AP correspondent's dis-patch was being put out from Paris Radio and being cabled to America for inclusion in the next morning's newspapers."

Here is the text of this dispatch :

"Allied air chiefs have made the long-awaited decision to adopt terror-bombings of German population centres as a ruthless ex-pedient of hastening Hitler's doom. More raids such as those recently carried out by heavy bombers of the Allied air forces on residential sections of Berlin, Dresden, Chemnitz and Kottbus are in store for the Germans for the avowed purpose of heaping more confusion on Nazi road and rail traffic, and to sap German morale. The all-out air war on Germany became obvious with the unprecedented daylight assault on the refugee-crowded capital, with civilians fleeing from the Red tide in the East.

"Thus, for one extraordinary moment, what might be termed the 'mask' of the Allied bomber commands appeared to have slipped. The dispatch—which was of course a hightly tendentious version of the Air Commodore's more moderate wording—was broadcast throughout liberated France and printed across America as front-page news; not only RAF Bomber Command—whose own air offensive had long been viewed with suspicion in the United States—but also their own US Strategic Air Forces were now delivering terror-raids on German civilians. At the time that the news broke in America, many people had only just finished listening incredulously to a radio message beamed across the Atlantic by German transmitters in which the big Berlin raid of 3rd February by the American bombers was condemned."

(D. Irving: *The Destruction of Dresden*, pp. 218–219)

David Irving continues:

"Now the vicious propaganda from Berlin was apparently being confirmed officially by an SHAEF announcement; British listeners were fortunately spared this dilemma: the British Government, which received news of the SHAEF press conference at 7.30 p.m. on the evening of 17th February, imposed a total press veto on publication of the dispatch soon after.

"The news was brought to General Eisenhower and General Arnold—both were gravely disturbed not only that the story had received such wide coverage, but also that an American air offensive which was, as they thought, directed only against precision military objectives, was being so manifestly misrepresented. General Arnold cabled Spaatz to check whether in fact there was any significant distinction between blind bombing by radar on military targets in urban areas, and 'terror' bombing, such as the SHAEF communiqué—as reported by Associated Press—claimed the Americans were now indulging in. General Spaatz replied, perhaps a shade cryptically, that he had not departed from the historical American policy in Europe—not even in the cases of the 3rd February Berlin raid or the 14th February Dresden raid. This discussion and its subsequent explanation satisfied General Arnold and the controversy was allowed to subside.

"General Spaatz had clearly eluded the onus of the responsibility for the Dresden raids and their consequences, but only just in time; his reassurance that the USSAF was attacking only military objectives, as always, pacified both Arnold and Eisenhower.

"The German Government, however, aware, in a way that neither the outside world nor indeed the German public could be, of what had really occurred in the Saxon capital, had no intention of relinquishing such a meaty propaganda detail. The very manner in which the report had been issued by SHAEF and then—as it was later—hastily stopped, the way in which the British Government alone had clamped a total ban on its publication, suggested that there was more to the Associated Press dispatch, which had by now reached Berlin through Sweden, than was superficially evident."

(D. Irving, op. cit., pp. 219–220)

On the military level, the matter would appear to have ended with the destruction of Dresden and with the massacre of approximately 135,000 civilian refugees, but it was to have profound repercussions in international diplomatic circles.

The German radio had already mentioned it, but there were more important developments than this. Foreign and neutral, particularly Swiss and Swedish, nationals, had witnessed the crime, and their accounts of the horrifying massacre they had witnessed were published in the world press. Public opinion rose in a volume which surprised the British and American Governments, and in England a number of eminent people persisted in demanding from the government an answer to a number of precise and highly embarrassing questions: Dr. Bell, Bishop of Chichester, the Very Rev. W. R. Inge, Deans of St. Paul's, Lord Hankey, who subsequently wrote a famous work entitled Politics, Trials and Errors, and the Labour Member of Parliament, Richard Stokes.

"On 6th March the German propaganda campaign achieved in London a success it could hardly have hoped for before: the occasion was the first full-scale debate on the air offensive since February 1944 when the Bishop of Chichester had raised the whole issue of area bombing of civilian targets in Europe.

"This time, when Mr. Richard Stokes took the floor at 2.43 p.m., he had the advantage of a British public more sympathetic towards the question than previously. Although Dr. Bell, the Bishop of Chichester, is known to have received hundreds of letters supporting his stand in the House of Lords, at the time of his speech in February 1944, he had been debating at the height of the Baby Blitz, and London opinion had been against him.

"Now in March 1945, with the end of the war heaving into sight, and with only the V2 threat hanging over it, the public was more vulnerable to the horrific descriptions of the consequences of these raids now being retailed in the British daily newspapers by correspondents in Geneva and Stockholm. As Mr. Stokes rose to speak, the Secretary for Air, Sir Archibald Sinclair, pointedly rose from his seat and left the Chamber; he refused to be drawn back, even when Stokes called attention to his absence. Richard Stokes was therefore obliged to commence his speech, one of the most telling in the history of the air offensive against Germany, without as it were the most prominent witness for the defence present.

"In his speech he returned to the theme he had been representing consistently since 1942; he was not convinced by the Minister's repeated insistence on the precision of Bomber Command's attacks; he also doubted the advantage of what he announced he would call 'strategic bombing', and commented that it was very noticeable that the Russians did not seem to indulge in 'blanket bombing'. He could see the advantage of their being able to say that it was the Western capitalist states which had perpetrated all these dirty tricks, while the Soviet Air Force had limited its bombing activities to what Mr. Stokes called 'tactical bombing'. In making this observation he was displaying remarkable prescience as the post-war years have demonstrated.

"The question was whether at this stage of the war the indiscriminate bombing of large population centres was a wise policy; he read to the House an extract from a report in the *Manchester Guardian*—based on a German telegraphic dispatch—which contained the remark that tens of thousands of Dresdeners were now buried under the ruins of the city, and that even an attempt at identification of the victims was proving hopeless.

"Stokes observed caustically that it was strange that the Russians seemed to be able to take great cities without blasting them to pieces, and added a question which clearly set even the Prime Minister's mind at work. 'What are you going to find', he asked, 'with all the cities blasted to pieces and with disease rampant? May not the disease, filth and poverty which will arise be almost impossible either to arrest or to overcome? I wonder very much whether it is realized at this stage. When I heard the Minister (Sir Archibald Sinclair) speak of the crescendo of destruction, I thought: what a magnificent expression for a Cabinet Minister of Great Britain at this stage of the war'.

"Stokes called attention to the Associated Press dispatch from the SHAEF Headquarters, and indeed read it out in full, thereby putting it on record for posterity; he asked once again the question he had asked so often before: Was terror-bombing now part of official Government policy? If so, then why was the SHAEF decision released and then suppressed? And why was it that in spite of the reports having been broadcast from Radio Paris, printed throughout America, and even being relayed back to the German people, the British people 'are the only ones who may not know what is being done in their name?' It was complete hypocrisy to say one thing and do another. In conclusion Mr. Stokes asserted that the British Government would live to rue the day that it had permitted these raids, and that the raids would stand for all time as 'a blot on our escutcheon'.

"One curious aspect of the SHAEF dispatch riddle remained unsolved: When the Associated Press dispatch was circulated and objections were raised in London to its publication, the first reaction from SHAEF was that it could not be suppressed, *as it represented official SHAEF policy* (Irving's italics). To this remark, backed up by the promise of documentary evidence, Sir Archibald Sinclair felt obliged to reply: the report certainly was not true, and Mr. Stokes might take that from him.

"Thus ended the last war-time debate on Bomber Command's policy; the British Government had been able to safeguard its secret from the day that the first area raid had been launched on Mannheim on 16th December 1940, right up to the end of the war.

"The creation of a scapegoat who could convincingly be blamed for the brutality of the bombing offensive presented few difficulties, now that the prime necessity for the bomber weapon was past. . . . On 28th March the Prime Minister signed a minute on the subject of the continued air offensive against German cities, and addresesd it to his Chiefs of Staff: he was clearly deeply impressed by reports reaching the Government of the shock waves still coursing through the civilized world about the attacks on the Eastern population centres:

"It seems to me, he wrote, that the moment has come when the question of bombing German cities simply for the sake of increasing the terror, though under other pretexts, should be reviewed. Otherwise we shall come into control of an utterly ruined land. We shall not, for instance, be able to get housing materials out of Germany for our own needs because some temporary provision would have to be made for the Germans themselves. The destruction of Dresden remains a serious query against the conduct of Allied bombing. I am of the opinion that military objectives must henceforward be more strictly studied in our own interests rather than that of the enemy . . . and I feel the need for more precise concentration upon military objectives. . . .

"This was indeed a remarkable document. Two possible interpretations were placed upon it at the time by those who learned of its contents: either the minute was hastily penned in the heat and turmoil of great events, and at a time when the Prime Minister was under considerable personal strain, simply recording the lessons learned from the aftermath of Dresden; or it could be construed as a carefully-phrased attempt at burdening for posterity the responsibility for the Dresden raids on to his Chiefs of Staff, and, perhaps more appositely, on to Bomber Command and Sir Arthur Harris.

"Sir Robert Saundby, Harris's Deputy at High Wycombe . . . recalls clearly the surprise and consternation felt by the Air Staff at what they felt to be implied by the Prime Minister: that he had been deliberately misled by his military advisers. What the Air Staff found most surprising, Saundby later related, was the suggestion that Bomber Command had been waging a purely terror offensive on its own initiative, 'though under other pretexts'.

"To the Chiefs of Staff, said Saundby, it looked as though it was an attempt on the Prime Minister's part to pretend that he had never ordered, or even advocated, that sort of thing. It was felt that it was not a fair picture of the Prime Minister to put on record, in view of what he had previously said and done. He was rather given to these impetuous flashes which were all very well in conversation, but not in a written minute. It might have led people to suppose that the Prime Minister himself had been misled by his military advisers to acquiescing in a policy of terror-bombing, because they had dressed it up in 'military' garments.

"In the face of the Air Staff's objection to his first minute, the Prime Minister wrote a second one, more circumspectly worded than the first. It omitted any direct reference either to Dresden on the one hand, or to the advantage of terror-bombing to the enemy on the other.

"The Prime Minister in his memoirs deals with the tragedy of the Dresden massacre in the following words: we made a heavy raid later in the month on Dresden, then a centre of communications of Germany's Eastern front. No attempt was made to depict the scale of the personal tragedies inflicted on the city, nor the controversial background and consequences to the raid."

In reply to a criticism of his role in Bomber Command in 1960, Sir Arthur Harris stated:

"The strategy of the bomber force which Earl Attlee criticizes was decided by HM Government, of which he (Attlee) was for most of the war a leading member. The decision to bomb industrial cities for morale effect was made, and in force, before I became C-in-C Bomber Command.

"No Commander-in-Chief", comments Irving, "would have been authorized to make such decisions, however adept he may have proved himself in their execution."

(D. Irving: The Destruction of Dresden, pp. 225–233)

To conclude our analysis of this policy of terror-bombing aimed at the destruction of civilian populations, we must briefly examine two points.

First of all, there is the question of responsibility. Despite all the precautions taken by the British Government and by SHAFE in order to hide the real truth for as long as possible, the truth did in the end filter out and the bombing of Dresden raised indignant reactions in the civilized world. Surprised at their unexpected violence, the Government sought a scape-goat in the person of Air Marshal Sir Arthur Harris. But the men who were indirectly responsible for the plan behind the scenes were the real culprits, and they were, firstly, Lindemann, who drew up the plan, and then Churchill, who accepted it, and finally the heads of the Government and of SHAFE, all of whom approved the policy at the same time as denying in public that it was being carried out.

Finally, it remains to consider the efficacity of the terror-bombing campaign. Although it is difficult to arrive at exact figures, the bombing raids on German towns is estimated to have caused six hundred thousand deaths and eight hundred thousand wounded. The blitz on London, which lasted several months, caused fifteen thousand civilian deaths and destroyed five hundred acres of buildings; by contrast the Allied raid on Hamburg caused fifty thousand deaths, and the bombing of Dresden, which lasted uninterrupted for thirty-six hours, killed one hundred and thirty-five thousand people and destroyed more than three thousand acres of buildings.

If the secret intent of these raids was an act of vengeance to satisfy the Jews by killing the greatest possible number of civilians, they may be regarded as a success. But they were a total failure as regards the following two vital points :

In the first instance, the promoters of the policy of terror-bombing intended that it should be used as a means to force the German population to sue for mercy, or even to provoke a rising against Hitler. On the contrary, it had the completely opposite effect, and only served to galvanize the Germans into a greater spirit of resistance and determination to stand by their Fuhrer.

The revelation of the Morgenthau and Kauffman plans, the Declaration of Casablanca, which demanded the unconditional surrender of Germany, the fatal Yalta Agreement, the unconditional support given to the Russians by Roosevelt and Eisenhower, and finally the terror-bombing raids—all these factors served to convince the German people that defeat would spell total annihilation of their country, and accordingly the whole people rose up with a desperate energy and fought to an absolute standstill. As a result, the war was unnecessarily prolonged for a further utterly profitless year, except that hundreds of thousands more men met their death, destruction took place on an appalling scale, but most important of all, this delay enabled the Russians to occupy half of Europe and thereby constitute a permanent menace to western civilization.

Secondly, the bombing raids were supposed to lead indirectly to the destruction of the German war industries. But one of the things which astonished the Allies when they occupied Germany after the war was to find that her industrial power had hardly been affected, for in this field they had accomplished veritable prodigies, and it is a fact that their war production never ceased to rise between 1939 and 1945. Following the terrible raid on Hamburg, war production in the area fell by fifty per cent, but only one month later it had risen to its original level. Five days after the destruction of Dresden the Germans had reopened the railway lines, which were used principally to evacuate the wounded and refugees from the Russian front.

Here is another significant detail. The tonnage of submarines launched in 1944 was greater than that of two years earlier. But in March 1945, when Germany was already partially invaded and was being bombed almost continuously day and night, more than 28,000 tons of submarines were being built monthly, as against 30,000 tons for the whole of 1941.

Again, in 1944 the aircraft industry produced more machines than at any time in the war: 40,593, as against 10,247 in 1940 and 12,401 in 1941.

Two factors considerably hampered the German war effort. They were terribly short of food and fuel, whereas the Allies could draw on abundant supplies of either, and secondly, towards the end of the war the Allies adopted a specialized pattern of bombing raids designed to destroy certain factories of absolutely vital importance: ball-bearing industries, petrol refineries, scientific research laboratories and test workshops for new engines such as the V1 and V2 at Peenemunde.

It is obvious that without ball-bearings and petrol one can neither manufacture nor put in service the aircraft, tanks and submarines that are indispensable for modern warfare. If this policy of specialized raids had been adopted from the outset it would have achieved far greater effect than the terror-bombing, and as a result the war would have been considerably shortened.

But those responsible for American policy seem to have been determined to prolong the war to allow the Russians to occupy that half of Europe which had been promised to them by Roosevelt at Yalta.

The German writer Karl Bartz has very clearly summed up the question of the efficacity of the terror-bombing in his book *Quand le ciel était en feu*:

"One of the key industries at the heart of all the German activity was the production of ball-bearings. If these factories had been destroyed, inevitably Germany would have been paralysed. No one knows why the Allies hesitated so long before attacking them. Their destruction would certainly have been much more useful than the destruction of three hundred towns (p. 282).

"The Allies could have shortened the war by at least a year and a half if they had wanted to. . . . By the end of 1944 petrol shortage was so severe that tanks could no longer be used during the offensive in the Ardennes. Similarly, if centres of fuel production had been attacked at the right moment, the war could have been brought to an end much more swiftly."

(K. Bartz: *Quand le ciel était en feu*, pp. 363-365)

By the end of April 1945, Germany had been invaded on every side, all her principal towns had been destroyed, and she was cut off from her basic resources. In such a situation it was impossible to continue the struggle, and on 30th April Hitler committed suicide in his bunker at Berlin, and his successor, Grand Admiral Doenitz, signed the order for unconditional surrender demanded by the victors on 7th May, to take effect from midnight 9th May.

VI

THE NUREMBERG TRIAL

We have already made several references to the question of responsibility, and this leads us to consider the war crimes trials, of which Nuremberg was the most celebrated and the most spectacular.

One of the essential clauses imposed on the defeated nation was that the political and military leaders of the Hitler regime, who were regarded as war criminals, should be brought to judgement.

The Allies are very proud of this innovation, which in principle was intended to punish war crimes and which, it was claimed, would establish a reign of Right and Justice in the world in future, thus serving to prevent the outbreak of new conflicts. The theory sounded magnificent, but in practice, the Nuremberg Trial, which served as the basis for numerous other processes, was a sinister and macabre farce. Proof of this is so abundant and obvious that we will simply confine ourselves to a brief resumé.

Let us first of all establish its origin in history. It is Dr. Nahum Goldmann, President of the World Jewish Congress, who claims for himself and for his Congress the honour of having first expounded the idea of setting up a court of justice for the purpose of punishing Nazi war criminals. This is what he says:

"The World Jewish Congress established the Institute of Jewish Affairs, where the groundwork was laid for two main objectives: ensuring that the Nazi criminals did not escape punishment and obtaining maximum restitution from a defeated Germany. It was in this Institute that the idea of punishing Nazi war criminals was first conceived, an idea later taken up by some great American jurists, notably Justice Robert H. Jackson of the Supreme Court, and implemented in the Nuremberg Trials. The idea of prosecuting and sentencing political and military leaders for crimes against humanity was completely new in international justice. Many jurists, unable to see beyond the concepts of conventional juris-prudence, were dubious or categorically opposed to it; also, the principle that one cannot be punished for a crime not prohibited by law at the time it is committed and that subordinates cannot be penalized for carrying out the orders of their superiors, seemed to argue against it. But these arguments were outweighed by the importance of exacting retribution for the Nazi regime's monstrous crimes against Jews and gentiles. The precedents had to be established that national sovereignty is no defence against infringements of the most basic principles of humanity, and obedience to a superior is not a valid excuse for individual and mass crimes. From this point of view the Nuremberg Trials were a momentous event in the history of international justice and morality. Not only did they prove their worth in bringing the top Nazi criminals to justice; they also served as an effective warning and deterrent for the future. Under the direction of Jacob and Nehemiah Robinson the World Jewish Congress put great effort into the intellectual and moral groundwork for these trials, and it is one of the triumphs of the Roosevelt administration that it consistently accepted these principles despite all the misgivings of some influential Allied circles, particularly in England."

(Dr. Nahum Goldmann : Memories, pp. 216-217)

The idea of these trials was launched by Nahum Goldmann in his opening speech at the Pan-American Conference of the World Jewish Congress, which was held at Baltimore in 1941. It was very carefully studied and perfected by the World Jewish Congress between 1942 and 1943, and then imposed on the American Government with the enthusiastic support of Roosevelt and his entourage.

The fate of the German leaders under the Hitler regime seems to have been discussed in public for the first time at the Teheran Conference in November 1943, and three years later, Elliott Roosevelt, the son of the American President, who was present at the banquet which was given by Stalin at the end of the Conference, published a very detailed account of the exchanges which took place during the conversation on that occasion, and from which we have taken the following passages :

"Toward the end of the meal Uncle Joe arose to propose his umpteenth toast . . . and it was on the subject of Nazi war criminals. I cannot hope to remember his words exactly, but it ran something like this :

" 'I propose a salute to the swiftest possible justice for all Germany's war criminals—justice before a firing squad. I drink to our unity in dispatching them as fast as we capture them, all of them, and there must be at least fifty thousand of them.'

"Quick as a flash Churchill was on his feet. (By the way, the

PM stuck to his favourite brandy throughout the toasting; his nightly regimen of cognac prepared him well for Russian-style conversation, but that night I suspect that even such a redoubtable tippler as he was finding his tongue thicker than usual.) His face and neck were red.

" 'Any such attitude', he cried, 'is wholly contrary to our British sense of justice! The British people will never stand for such mass murder. I take this opportunity to say that I feel most strongly that no one, Nazi or no, shall be summarily dealt with, before a firing squad, without proper legal trial, no matter what the known facts and proven evidence against him!'

"I glanced at Stalin: he seemed hugely tickled, but his face remained serious; only his eyes twinkled as he took up the PM's challenge and drew him on, suavely pricking his arguments, seemingly careless of the fact that Churchill's temper was now hopelessly lost. At length, Stalin turned to Father and asked *his* opinion. Father, who had been hiding a smile, nevertheless felt that the moment was beginning to be too highly charged with bad feeling: it was his notion to inject a witticism.

" 'As usual,' he said, 'it seems to be my function to mediate this dispute. Clearly there must be some sort of compromise between your position, Mr. Stalin, and that of my good friend the Prime Minister. Perhaps we could say that, instead of summarily executing fifty thousand war criminals, we should settle on a smaller number. Shall we say forty-nine thousand five hundred?'

"Americans and Russians laughed. The British, taking their cue from their Prime Minister's mounting fury, sat quiet and straight-faced. Stalin, on top of the situation, pursued Father's compromise figure; he asked around the table for agreement of new estimates. The British were careful: The subject requires and deserves a great deal of study, they said. The Americans, on the other hand, were more jocular: Let's brush it off—we're still miles and miles and months and months away from Germany and conquest of the Nazis. I was hoping that Stalin would be satisfied by the early answers, and change the subject before he got to me, but if he is anything, he is persistent. The question came. Somewhat uncertainly I got to my feet.

" 'Well,' I said, and took a deep breath, trying to think fast through the champagne bubbles. 'Isn't the whole thing pretty academic? Look: when our armies start rolling in from the west, and your armies are still coming on from the east, we'll be solving the whole thing, won't we? Russian, American, and British soldiers will settle the issue for most of those fifty thousand, in battle, and I hope that not only those fifty thousand war criminals will be taken care of, but many hundreds of thousands more Nazis as well.' And I started to sit down again.

"But Stalin was beaming with pleasure. Around the table he came, flung an arm around my shoulders. An excellent answer! A toast to my health! I flushed with pleasure, and was about to drink, for it is the Russian custom for one to drink even when it is his own health that is proposed, when all of a sudden an angry finger was being waved right in my face.

" 'Are you interested in damaging relations between the Allies? Do you know what you are saying? How can you dare say such a thing?' It was Churchill—and he was furious, and no fooling. Somewhat shaken to find the Prime Minister and the Marshal squabbling right over my head and feeling a little like Alice-in-Wonderland being crowded by the Hatter and the March Hare at the celebrated Tea Party, I regained my chair, and sat quiet, worried stiff.

"Fortunately the dinner broke up soon afterward, and I followed Father back to his apartment to apologize. After all, damaging relations between the Allies!

"Father roared with laughter. 'Don't think a second about it,' he insisted. 'What you said was perfectly all right. It was fine. Winston just lost his head when everybody refused to take the subject seriously. Uncle Joe . . . the way he was needling him, he was going to take offence at what anybody said, specially if what was said pleased Uncle Joe. Don't worry, Elliott.'

" 'Because *you* know . . . the last thing I'd. . . .'

" 'Forget it,' said Father, and laughed again. 'Why, Winston will have forgotten all about it when he wakes up.'

"But I don't think he ever did forget it. All the months I was to be stationed in England, later on, I was never again invited to spend the night at Chequers. Apparently Mr. Churchill never forgets."

(E. Roosevelt : *As He Saw It*, pp. 188–191)

"Thus began", as Mr. Veale observes in his remarkable book *Advance to Barbarism* (p. 216), "the first exchange of views on the then startling and seemingly original suggestion that, after a victory, there ought to be a grand massacre of the vanquished.

"There is, of course, no obligation to accept Elliott's story as an accurate, objective account of what took place that evening in Teheran, since it is obviously written to glorify President Roosevelt's statecraft, urbanity, and tact at the expense of Mr. Churchill, whom Elliott evidently heartily disliked. Still, in its main outlines, no doubt, Elliott's story should be accepted as approximately accurate . . . and what he says took place at Teheran is entirely consistent with what we all know took place later.

(F. J. P. Veale, ibid., pp. 217–218)

"Six years after the publication of Elliott Roosevelt's version, however, an alternative account of this episode has become available from the pen of Mr. Winston Churchill himself, in the instalment of his War Memoirs entitled *Closing the Ring* (1952). True, Mr. Churchill complains that Elliott's version is 'highly coloured and extremely misleading', but in fact his own version confirms Elliott's account of the essential point of the story. At this banquet at Teheran, Mr. Churchill says that Stalin pointed out that Germany's strength depended upon 50,000 officers and technicians and, if these were rounded up and shot, 'German military strength would be extirpated'. In spite of Mr. Churchill's indignant protest, however, these 50,000 must be shot, Stalin insisted.

"The two versions therefore agree that a massacre of 50,000 persons when victory was achieved was proposed by Stalin at the Teheran Conference but, whereas Elliott says these 50,000 were to be 'war criminals', Churchill says they were to be the officers and technicians upon whom Germany's strength depended. . . . What Stalin clearly had in mind was a massacre similar to the Katyn Forest Massacre which the Soviet authorities had carried out only three and a half years before. . . . As a Marxist it was natural that Stalin should frame his proposal in the way in which Mr. Churchill says he framed it. It was equally natural that Elliott Roosevelt, knowing nothing of Marxian ideology, should quite guilelessly have assumed that Stalin must have intended to propose the mass execution of criminals, and so, without intending to mislead, he interpreted Stalin's words in his own bourgeois phraseology. (ibid., p. 219)

"It is fortunate that this incident has been recorded in such detail by two independent witnesses whose testimony is on the essential point so exactly in agreement. . . ." In the event, "the Soviet Government proved most accommodating: so long as liquidation was reached in the end, it was of no consequence what preliminary judicial fooleries were indulged in to satisfy capitalist susceptibilities. . . . Ultimately, the American solution was carried out; Stalin had his mass murder and Mr. Churchill his trial."

(F. J. P. Veale, ibid., pp. 218, 220, 224)

The Nuremberg Trial served as a prototype for numerous other War Crimes Trials of which the most important, although it was hardly reported in the European press, was the great Tokyo Trial. The trial of the German war criminals opened at Nuremberg on 20th November 1945, under an American President, Justice R. H. Jackson of the Supreme Court of the United States. America bore the cost of the trials, it was Americans who guarded the prisoners, and the executioner was an American. In other words, it was America, with Jewish and Soviet support behind the scenes, who bore the responsibility for the trial.

In his opening speech, Mr. Justice Robert H. Jackson, Chief Prosecutor for the United States, stated:

"We would make clear that we have no purpose to incriminate the whole German people. . . . If the German populace had willingly accepted the Nazi programme, no Storm-troopers would have been needed in the early days of the Party, and there would have been no need for concentration camps and the Gestapo."
(*The Trial of Major German War Criminals*, HMSO, 1946, p. 6)

"Any resort to war—to any kind of war—is a resort to means that are inherently criminal. War inevitably is a course of killings, assaults, deprivations of liberty and destruction of property (ibid., p. 39). . . . The Charter recognizes that one who has committed criminal acts may not take refuge in superior orders nor in the doctrine that his crimes were acts of State. These twin principles, working together, have heretofore resulted in immunity for practically everyone concerned in the really great crimes against peace and mankind (ibid., p. 42) . . . the ultimate step in avoiding periodic wars, which are inevitable in a system of international lawlessness, is to make statesmen responsible to law. And let me make clear that while this law is first applied against German aggressors, the law includes, and if it is to serve a useful purpose it must condemn, aggression by any other nations, including those which sit here now in judgment." (ibid., p. 45).

These are fine sentiments, but they are nevertheless difficult to put into practice.

The act of indictment was divided into four main counts:

1. The crime of conspiracy,
2. Crimes against peace,
3. War crimes,
4. Crimes against humanity.

These accusations were thought up by the Americans, but up to the present time they are unrecognized in international law. Besides, they were new and ill-defined notions that were not at all easy to proceed upon.

The Tribunal was composed of the following members: The United States were represented by Justice Jackson and ten assistants. The chief British prosecutor was the Attorney-General, Sir Hartley Shawcross, assisted by the Lord Chancellor, Jowitt, and eleven assistants. France was represented by Robert Falco, a barrister of the Court of Appeal, and Professor Andre Gros, a specialist in international law, and for the Soviet Union there was General T. Nikitchenko, vice-president of the Supreme Court of Moscow, and two assistants.

The deliberations which preceded the opening of the Nuremberg Trials were held in the greatest secrecy in London. At first, everything went wrong, so wrong, in fact, that on several occasions it seemed as if the discussions would end in failure. The result of these labours was the London Agreement, which was made public on 8th August 1945, but the details of the sessions, which were not published until four years later, revealed serious differences of opinion, and indeed it was evident that certain problems seemed insoluble:

1. What would be the attitude of the Tribunal if the German defence raised the question of wars of aggression and crimes committed by other nations?

2. How was one to justify the accusation and condemnation of certain men whose acts, given the state of the law at that time, could not be considered as crimes?

3. By creating new precedents, would not the victorious countries lay themselves open to similar charges in turn in the future?

4. Should the ticklish question of aerial attacks against defenceless towns and civilian populations be brought up?

And this was not all. At that time London was swarming with refugees from Estonia, Lithuania, Latvia and Poland. These exiles were vigorously opposed to permitting the Russians holding a seat on the future international court. In their opinion, Russia, who had dismembered Poland and commenced wars of aggression against Finland and the Baltic States, ought to be sitting with the accused and not among the judges.

The British delegation was also troubled by the possibility that the German defence would represent the occupation of Norway as a legitimate act of defence, which could be a source of embarrassment. But Jackson had already found a way of overcoming this reef. A clause would be inserted in the statutes of the Tribunal limiting the extent of the trial simply to the consideration of acts committed by the accused. In other words, the criticism or even the discussion of the acts of the victorious governments was formally forbidden. Another problem was that of responsibility, or more exactly, personal responsibility. Relatively easy to sort out when it was a matter of Goering or Frank, it became extremely delicate in the case of certain technicians such as Schacht, for example, the financial expert, who had no part in any crime or in any infraction of international law.

Most of these criticisms and objections were perfectly valid, as the future was to show, but the Americans had their way, and on the heels of the London Agreement, which was drawn up between the British, American, French and Russian Governments to establish a body to be called the International Military Tribunal for the trial of the "major war criminals whose offences have no particular geographical location", the Nuremberg Trial opened on 20th November 1945. On 30th September 1946, after 407 sessions, the verdict was pronounced. Twelve of the accused were sentenced to death: Goering, Ribbentrop, Keitel, Kaltenbrunner, Rosenberg, Frick, Frank, Streicher, Sauckel, Jodl, Seyss-Inquart and, in his absence, Martin Bormann.

Hess, Funk and Raeder were condemned to life imprisonment, and Schirach and Speer got twenty years, Neurath fifteen, and Doenitz ten, Schacht, von Papen and Fritzsche were acquitted. Those condemned to death were executed in the night of 15th to 16th October, but two hours before the execution was due to take place, Goering committed suicide in his cell with a cyanide pill. It was never discovered how he had managed to get hold of it.

The criticisms that can be raised against the Nuremberg Trials and the numerous other trials to which it gave birth are so numerous, so evident and so irrefutable that it will suffice if we just resume them here briefly.

1. At Nuremberg, it was not a question of a neutral and impartial tribunal; it was a court of the conquerors sitting in judgment on the leaders of a vanquished country, who had no right of appeal.

2. The notion of "war crimes" such as established at Nuremberg is an entirely new conception which until then had not existed in any known code of laws. War crimes, crimes against peace, crimes against humanity and crimes of conspiracy are decidedly vague terms, very difficult to define and susceptible of very varied interpretations.

3. When acts which may be regarded as "war crimes" had been committed simultaneously by the Germans and by the Allies, either they were not regarded as crimes, and were never brought up at

Nuremberg, as was the case with the aerial bombardments, for example, or else the Germans were condemned and the Allies were automatically absolved if not glorified since, according to Justice Jackson, it was forbidden to criticize or even to discuss the acts of the victorious governments. In other words, at Nuremberg the unforgivable crime was to be on the side of the vanquished.

4. Unconditional obedience to one's superior's orders was regarded as a crime at Nuremberg, when these orders were held to be contrary to morality or to national interest, but unconditional obedience was required on the Allied side, or at least was considered as a perfectly valid excuse in the case of misdemeanours committed on their side. Besides, military discipline is impossible and no army could exist if the lower ranks were allowed to debate their orders.

5. At Nuremberg and at the trials which followed thereafter, any number of sentences were passed based upon retroactive considerations, or in other words, they were condemned for acts which were in no way considered as crimes or offences at the time when they had committed them, and this is contrary to the most elementary principles of law and to the most ancient traditions of legal practice.

6. The presence of the Russians among the judges at Nuremberg was a bitter mockery and a permanent violation of all principles of justice, since Soviet Russia alone has been responsible for more crimes than any other European country, including Hitler's Germany.

7. Under the label of "war criminals" there were lumped together regardless in one group, an assortment of Hitler's thugs, misled idealists, servile courtesans, and heroic soldiers and sailors whose conduct had been irreproachable.

8. The whole world now knows, as Field-Marshal Montgomery has pointed out, that at the end of the next war, the political and military leaders of the vanquished countries will be executed in the manner determined by the customs of the victors. We have stepped back to the epoch of Attila and Genghis Khan, when the victors automatically massacred their enemy. That will not help to lessen bloody wars nor to reduce the severity of the strife.

One of the capital mistakes committed by the Allies at Nuremberg was to equate the Wehrmacht with the Nazi party and thus render the German Generals responsible for the extortions and wrongs of the regime. In fact there always existed a fundamental antagonism between the Wehrmacht leaders and the Nazi party. The German Generals, who had been schooled in the traditional discipline of the old imperial army, regarded Hitler as a low-class upstart, and reproached him for lowering political morality to the level of gangsterism and discrediting Germany in the eyes of the civilized nations.

Hitler, who felt that they secretly despised him, hated and distrusted his generals, especially when they belonged to the old German military aristocracy. But he could not dispense with them, and hence his anger, which at times gave vent to outbursts of uncontrolled fury.

This antagonism increased in proportion as the situation worsened on all fronts, and when it became evident that Hitler's presence at the head of the government was leading Germany to catastrophe, there was only one solution: to get rid of Hitler. Unfortunately, however, obedience and discipline are as second nature in the German army, and only a desperate situation would urge the generals to open rebellion. Besides, public opinion in Germany would have to be taken into account if it was to succeed; but the public, intoxicated by Goebbels' propaganda, completely misunderstood the situation and blindly trusted in its Fuhrer. On top of that, one has to take into account Roosevelt's pro-Soviet policy—the Morgenthau Plan, Germany's total and unconditional surrender, and the surrender of half of Europe to the Soviets—a crazy policy from the European point of view, which made the whole situation even more complicated, since the German generals were patriots, and they were not prepared to sacrifice Hitler merely in order to hand over Germany bound hand and foot into Soviet tyranny. It was a formidable situation to be resolved.

Several attempts to assassinate Hitler failed at the last moment owing to unforeseen circumstances. On 20th July 1944 Hitler had a miraculous escape, and following this attempt a great number of officers and politicians were massacred, including some of the most famous leaders of the German army: Colonel Count von Stauffenberg, a war hero of the Afrika Corps who was covered with wounds, and who had been the mainspring of the plot, and Marshals Rommel, von Witzleben, and von Kluge, Admiral Canaris, General von Stulpnagel, and others.

It cannot be denied that on Hitler's express orders the war in the East was conducted with an extreme savagery for which the German army was not responsible. The German generals had always protested against such barbarous methods of warfare, but Hitler took not the slightest note of them.

The English writer, John W. Wheeler-Bennett has clearly described the reaction of the German army's leaders to these barbarous orders in his book *The Drama of the Germany Army:*

"Quite a few of the generals who had campaigned in Poland were shattered by what they had seen. These men were normally

able to withstand the horrors of war, but they were not prepared
for the abominations engendered by the Nazi ideology. When they
had heard their Fuhrer speaking of 'extermination' at Obersalzberg
on 22nd August, they imagined that he was being carried away
by force of oratory and by his imagination. When he had said:
'our strength lies in the absence of all pity, and in violence' and
when he had spoken of 'mercilessly killing everyone of the Polish
race and tongue, men, women and children', they little imagined
that they were supposed to take these proposals literally, for-
getting that, except when he had given his word, Hitler always
thought what he spoke.

"It wasn't long before they discovered the terrible truth. The
Polish campaign had only been launched two weeks, and victory
was already in sight, when Ribbentrop informed Keitel, on the
Headquarters train on 12th September, of the Fuhrer's instructions
for dealing with the Polish question. These instructions included
massive executions among all the members of the intelligentzia,
the nobility and the clergy—in other words, among all the classes
capable of providing future leaders in the event of a resistance
movement—and a general massacre of the Jews.

"Keitel transmitted these instructions to Canaris, who was
absolutely confounded. The 'little Admiral' replied that such a
thing was impossible, and that German military honour would
be stained for all eternity if he were to allow such horrors to take
place. But Keitel replied that the Fuhrer had ordered that these
measures should be carried out, and furthermore, he had added that
if they were not to the army's liking, the army would have to
accept an equal number of SS and SIPO (security police) units, who
would carry out the Fuhrer's orders independently of the military
authorities. (This is in fact what happened one month later.)
Under these conditions, the armed forces of the Reich had no
choice but to obey the orders of their supreme commander. 'A
day will come', Canaris told Keitel with prophetic accuracy, 'when
the world will hold the Wehrmacht, under whose eyes these things
have been allowed to happen, responsible for these atrocious
measures'."

(op. cit., p. 389, translated from the French edition)

The same methods were applied even more strenuously against
the Russians, and it is virtually certain that this policy cost Hitler
the war, since, at the beginning, the German troops were frequently
greeted as liberators from the bolshevic tyranny. But Hitler was not
waging war against bolshevism but against the Russian nation and

against the Slav race, which was the greatest assistance to Stalin, whose regime, tottering on the edge of defeat, was thus consolidated. Hitler was massacring national élites in the name of the superior race, and Stalin was doing the same on his side in the name of a revolutionary morality which demanded the annihilation of social classes that could not be assimilated by Marxism. The war which this state of affairs produced attained apocalyptic depths of horror, but once again it was the Party and not the army which bore the responsibility.

Among the Nuremberg files is a document of capital importance. It is a secret report which was sent to Alfred Rosenberg by Dr. Brautigam on 24th October 1942. Rosenberg was the Nazi minister in charge of the administration of occupied territory in the East, and Dr. Bräutigam was political adviser to Marshals List and Kleist who were in command of the army on the Caucasian front.

In his report, Bräutigam sets out with great clarity and extra-ordinary frankness the main mistakes in Hitler's policy towards the Russian people. He does not hide the fact that such a savage attitude could cost Germany the war, and in fact this is precisely what happened. Here are the essential passages from this report:

"When we entered Soviet territory, we found a people exhausted by bolshevism, and desperately awaiting a new ideology which would bring them the hope of a better future. Germany's duty was to provide them with this ideology (Sic: formules), but this was not done. The people greeted us with joy as liberators, and willingly put themselves in our hands.

"But with the natural instinct of Eastern peoples, they soon discovered that for Germany the slogan 'liberation from bolshevism' was simply a pretext for reducing them to a new slavery. . . . Peasants and working-men soon understood that Germany did not regard them as partners possessing equal rights, but simply as the object of her own political and economic ideals. With unequalled presumption . . . we treated the people of occupied Eastern ter-ritories as 'second-class whites', whom Providence had assigned to Germany alone as her slaves. . . .

"It is no secret that our Russian prisoners died of hunger and cold by the hundreds of thousands. As a result. we are now in the absurd position of having to recruit millions of workmen in the occupied territories of the East, having allowed thousands of prisoners of war to die of hunger like flies. . . .

"With the fathomless scorn of the prevailing Slav mentality, methods of 'recruiting' were employed whose origins doubtless go back to the darkest periods of the slave trade. A veritable man-hunting campaign was instigated. Without any consideration for their age or physical condition, people were sent into Germany.

"Our policy forced both the bolshevics and the Russian nation-alists to combine against us, and today Russia is fighting with a courage and an exceptional spirit of sacrifice simply in order that its human dignity should be recognized."

Naturally this report was completely ignored. Hitler, Rosenberg and Himmler, who were all in favour of adopting a tough line vis-à-vis the Slavs, would not hear of it. Goebbels was indeed aware of the errors being committed, but he was powerless against the other three.

The generals of the Wehrmacht reacted as best they could. But Hitler forbade them to interfere in politics, and they had all their time taken up in conducting the war without being concerned about other matters such as this.

The historian, J. de Launay, in his *La Guerre Psychologique*, clearly demonstrated the efforts the Wehrmacht made to counter-balance Hitler's policy :

"The first reception accorded by the 'liberated' Russian peoples to the Wehrmacht had been favourable, and all the heads in the army recommended a policy of collaboration. Lieutenant Colonel Gehlen even proposed that 200,000 Russian volunteers, who wanted to serve in the German army, should be armed. Gehlen, like Colonel Count Stauffenberg, thought that in order to conquer Russia, it was necessary to co-operate with the Russians while liberating them from the Soviet system. But Keitel informed them on several occasions that 'the Fuhrer did not want politics in the armed forces'.

"The Russian prisoners of war were maltreated, and they turned to resistance. Nevertheless, Stauffenberg and Bräutigam en-deavoured to find a 'Russian de Gaulle'. Marshal von Bock approved a plan for creating a 'liberation army' of 200,000 Russian volunteers, but Bock was dismissed in the autumn of 1941 and his successor, Marshal von Kluge, did not dare to raise the question with the Fuhrer.

"In September 1941 the municipal council of Smolensk, which had recently been set up by the Germans, had demanded per-mission to form a free Russian government, but Keitel's reply, which was received in November, had been a categorical refusal.

"Thereafter there was a succession of individual initiatives :

General von Schenkendorff decided to form six Russian battalions under the command of the Cossack Kononow, in order to protect the railway lines to the rear of the armies in the central group. General Schmidt, commander of the second tank army, set up a self-governing Russian district (Lokotj) under the leadership of a former Russian mayor, Kaminski. Later, Kaminski, who had been made a brigade commander, formed his own army.

"The Reichskommissariat, on the other hand, pursued their punitive action, openly firing upon the people, and provoking resistance movements.

"The propaganda service of the Wehrmacht, under the direction of General von Wedel, attempted to redress the balance, and even considered adopting a scheme of agrarian reform. A Russian emigré, Kasanzew, was put in charge of drawing up leaflets and publishing a propaganda newspaper, but there again Keitel blocked all these efforts.

"In August 1942, at the time the German armies were conquering the Caucasus, a new hope arose, when General Köstring, the former military attaché at Moscow, was appointed adviser to Marshal List. Bräutigam was his political adviser, and he recommended to List and his successor, Kleist, a certain degree of co-operation with the Russians. Rosenberg had promised Bräutigam that labour forces would not be conscripted for work in Germany from the Caucasians, and that the rapid dissolution of the kolkhozes was envisaged. Accordingly, Köstring and Bräutigam were well received in the Caucasus, and even witnessed extraordinarily joyful 'liberation celebrations'. But after the defeat at Stalingrad, the Caucasian collaborators were compelled to flee, and they sought permission to join with the German army in its retreat. This was granted to Bräutigam by Marshal Kleist, but many who believed in the Germans' word were nevertheless abandoned.

"The whole of this operation is revealing of the flagrant contradiction which existed between certain of the Fuhrer's directives. On the one hand there was Rosenberg, carrying out a punitive policy by means of his unscruplous gauleiters, and on the other hand, Goebbels, the political idealist, was promising a better future. These deceiving claims, which were shown up every day by the facts of the occupation, certainly contributed to reuniting the Russian people against the invader.

"Psychologically, Germany's action in the East was a total failure. The Fuhrer alone bears the blame for this."
(*Les Dossiers de la Seconde Guerre Mondiale*, 5th part, "The Psychological War", by J. de Launay, 1964)

However, the Wehrmacht succeeded in reconstituting the Wlassof army, which had a considerable strength, but Hitler, who was extremely suspicious of this initiative, fanatically opposed its entry into the war, and as a result, it remained virtually inactive up to the end.

The Americans handed over the leaders of the Wlassof army to the Russians, who hanged them and sent their soldiers into labour and concentration camps.

While still on this subject, let us quote Admiral Doenitz's reaction, as Commander in Chief of the Navy, and Hitler's successor-designate, when he discovered the existence of Hitler's concentration camps:

"On 7th May, Friedeburg and Jodl returned to Mürwick. Friedeburg brought with him a copy of *Stars and Stripes*, an American military publication, which contained some appalling photographs taken in the concentration camp at Buchenwald. Doubtless, the disorganization of transport and the supply of food had not served to improve the conditions in these camps in the course of the last weeks; nevertheless, it was beyond question that nothing could justify the conditions that these photographs demonstrated. Friedeburg and myself were staggered. We would never have imagined that such things were possible! But they were indeed true—and not only at Buchenwald—as we realized for ourselves when a boat transporting detainees of a concentration camp arrived at Flensburg. The eldest naval officer did everything in his power to feed and care for these unfortunate people. How could such horrors have happened in Germany without being brought to our knowledge?

"Up to 1939, I had spent my whole time at sea, as Commander of the *Emden*, and then in charge of the submarines. As from the outbreak of war, I lived mainly at my command Headquarters, which were first at Sengwarden, in Eastern Frisia, and then at Paris and Lorient. These various places were a sort of military oasis. We had little or no contact with the German people. Technical problems and the conduct of submarine warfare absorbed all my time. The only information that came through to me from the enemy concerned submarines. As far as I was concerned there was no doubt that the enemy radio was and ought to be controlled for propaganda purposes, as ours was. Accordingly, I didn't listen to either.

"When I was put in command of the Navy, I usually stayed at my command post, 'Koralle', which was a lonely place between

Bernau and Eberswalde, to the north of Berlin. When I visited General Headquarters, I only took part in military conferences, and Hitler only consulted me on questions within my competence. Besides, as I have said, it was impossible to take any interest in anything else, since all my time was taken up in my work.

"The facts which I learnt about the inhuman side of the National Socialist regime in the months which followed the capitulation in 1946 exerted a profound influence over me. I have set out above my attitude towards the Party and my relations with Hitler. As I have said, the idea of a national community, in the proper, social sense of this word, and the cohesion of the German people upon this base, fired me with enthusiasm. Hitler's reunion of all the branches of the German race under one Reich seemed to me the achievement of one of the oldest dreams of our nation. Our dispersion can be traced back to the Treaty of West-phalia, which brought to an end the Thirty Years War. Our adversaries, who had achieved their own unity at the beginning of the modern era, wanted to keep us weak and to prevent us achieving our unity for a very long time. Only National Socialism had been able to overcome all these obstacles, and accordingly it has acquired immense historical value.

"But it was then that I learnt about its other aspects, which were infinitely less attractive, and as a result my attitude suddenly changed towards the regime which he (Hitler) had created.

"On 6th May, I relieved Himmler of all his functions. When I discovered all the facts relative to the concentration camps, I was sorry that I had let him off, since I was of the opinion that it was a purely German affair, and that we ourselves ought to bring to light all these atrocities, and ourselves punish those who were guilty. Count Schwerin-Krosigk was of exactly the same opinion. He sent me a decree ordering legal proceedings to be set up to enquire into these heinous crimes, and I sent a copy of the text of it to Eisenhower, requesting him to allow our judges every neces-sary facility for taking these steps. At an interview with General Murphy, the General's political adviser, I specifically brought this point to his attention and requested his support, which he promised me, but I never heard any more about the matter".

(Grand Admiral Doenitz: *Ten Years and Twenty Days*, translated from the French edition)

The Allies, who had barely understood what was happening in Germany during the war, thus committed a tragic error in equating the army with Hitler's regime. The condemnation at Nuremberg and

c

other places, of irreproachable leaders such as Doenitz, Raeder, von Kesselring and von Manstein, or of Yamashita at Tokyo, was a perfectly iniquitous and monumental act of injustice. Goering, Keitel and Jodl, on the other hand, could justly be considered as servile politicians, who were the accomplices of and co-responsible for the acts of the Party.

The Allies, however, did something infinitely worse than that. Their erroneous equation of the army with the Party in Germany, the policy of terror-bombing, the blindly pro-Soviet attitude of the Americans and their obstinacy in demanding global and unconditional surrender from Germany—all these factors combined to produce consequences of quite exceptional gravity. For as a result, the war was utterly needlessly prolonged for a further year and a half, hundreds of thousands more men were killed, and worst of all, the Soviets were enabled to occupy half Europe, in which they have become solidly entrenched, representing a far greater menace for the West than ever did Nazism.

Today the Americans are paying for the politically criminal and insane policy adopted by Roosevelt at Quebec, Teheran and Yalta, unless it can be said that he and his Jewish advisers actually intended to hand over Europe to Communism, a conclusion which would seem to be justified by the famous Morgenthau Documents.

In his Memoirs, Admiral Doenitz has clearly explained the tragic dilemma with which he found himself confronted when he was suddenly made responsible for Germany's future as Hitler's successor-designate.

"In January 1945 the German government entered into possession of the British instruction 'Eclipse' which dealt with 'Measures to be adopted for the occupation of Germany' after its unconditional surrender. A map, attached to the document, showed the division of the country between the Soviet Union, the United States and Great Britain. It corresponded to the future delineation of the zones of occupation, with the exception of the French zone, which was introduced at the Yalta Conference. This division, and the methods revealed in the Morgenthau Plan, caused us to fear for our future existence as a separate nation.

"The severity of these intentions strengthened our political opposition to the alternative of bringing a rapid end to hostilities by means of an unconditional surrender. Besides, there were other extremely important and practical considerations against adopting this course.

"On 12th January 1945, the Russians launched a new offensive.

They penetrated into Silesia and reached the middle bank of the Oder at Kustrin and Frankfurt. The Wehrmacht was unable to fulfil its natural mission of protecting our peoples in the East and their territory. Terrified masses fled towards the West. They knew what the Soviet invasion meant. In October 1944, having captured Goldap and several villages on the frontier of Eastern Prussia, they massacred their inhabitants with unheard of cruelty. An appeal to the Red Army by the Jewish writer, Ilya Ehrenburg, made it quite clear :

" 'Kill'. Kill ! In the German race there is nothing but evil; not one among the living, not one among the yet unborn but is evil ! Follow the precepts of Comrade Stalin. Stamp out the Fascist beast once and for all in its lair ! Use force and break the racial pride of the Germanic women. Take them as your lawful booty. Kill ! as you storm onwards, kill, you gallant soldiers of the Red Army !'

"In my opinion", continues Doenitz, "the first duty which befell what remained of our armed forces was to save these unfortunate peoples. If, to our great sorrow, we were unable to defend their lands, the very least we could do was to save their lives. If only for this reason, it was indispensable to pursue the struggle on the Eastern front.

"There is another factor to consider. At the behest of the Allies, the war could only be terminated by our unconditional surrender. As far as our troops were concerned, the signature of this capitulation would immediately arrest their movements. They would have to lay down their arms and hand themselves over, wherever they might be. If we had capitulated in the winter of 1944-1945, three and a half million soldiers, who were still very far from the Anglo-American front, would have been taken prisoner by the Russians. With the best will in the world the latter would have been incapable of looking after them, feeding and sheltering them. Our men would have had to camp out in the open and in the cold, and in consequence there would certainly have been an appalling mortality. What happened in May, at a much more favourable time, is proof of this. Even in the West, the English and the Americans were unable to provide enough food for their prisoners, large numbers of whom died.

"In consequence, the termination of the war by unconditional surrender during the winter of 1944-1945 would have entailed the death of millions of soldiers and civilians. None of those who then held a responsible position in the Wehrmacht could urge this course of action. None of the unfortunate refugees in the East would have agreed to being handed over to the Russians in this way, and no soldier wanted to endure Soviet captivity. The troops probably would not have obeyed the order to stop where they were and hand themselves in. No commander could have signed the capitulation at this period without knowing that it would not be respected and also that by so doing he would be consigning a large number of people to their destruction. . . . No one in conscience could take such a decision.

"Painful though it was to have to continue the struggle and sacrifice men on land and on sea, and accept the civilian losses caused by the bombing raids, nevertheless it had to be done because these sacrifices would in the end prove to be less than those which a premature surrender of the territories of the East would have entailed."

In the first days of May, Admiral Doenitz began direct negotiations with Field-Marshal Montgomery, with a view to concluding a partial German capitulation, limited to the English sector on the Western front, and independently of the Russian front. Montgomery laid down certain conditions before it could be accepted.

"On 4th May I gave Friedeburg full powers to accept Montgomery's demands. He left by aeroplane for the British Headquarters, with instructions to continue, after the convention had been signed, to Reims, where General Eisenhower was stationed, in order to offer a similar partial capitulation to the Americans. After his departure, we felt a burden had been taken off our shoulders. We had just taken the first step towards surrender in the West without having to agree to surrender our soldiers and civilians to the Russians. This had other consequences. Montgomery demanded the cessation of hostilities on the sea, and the surrender of ships which were in the waters of Holland, North-West Germany, Schleswig-Holstein and Denmark. Going one step further ahead, at midday on 4th May I ordered our submarines throughout the world to cease hostilities. This was part of my intention to cease hostilities against the West at the earliest possible moment.

"In the evening Friedeburg announced that he had signed the capitulation with Montgomery and that he was leaving to see Eisenhower. The capitulation took effect from eight o'clock on the morning of 5th May.

"On the morning of 6th May, General Kinzel, who had accompanied Friedeburg, arrived at Mürwick, having been sent by Friedeburg to inform me of the state of negotiations with Eisenhower. The latter, he told me, in contrast with Montgomery, refused to accept a partial capitulation under any conditions. We had to surrender now unconditionally, and on every front, including the Russian front. The troops were to lay down their arms, wherever they might be, to be taken prisoner. The High Command of the Wehrmacht would be responsible for seeing that this surrender was carried out, and the order extended to all ships of war and commerce.

"We were afraid that Eisenhower might adopt this attitude. In my speech on the wireless on 1st May, I had said: 'As from this moment, the British and the Americans are no longer fighting for their own countries, but for the extension of bolshevism in Europe'. An American station, situated at Eisenhower's General Headquarters, had replied that this was 'a typical and well-known trick of the Nazis in an endeavour to create a split between Eisenhower and his Russian allies'.

"However the latest operations which he had ordered showed that he was not in the least aware of the turn taken by world politics at that moment. After his troops had crossed the Rhine at Remagen, America had achieved her strategic object of conquering Germany. From this moment the paramount objective should have become political, namely, the occupation of the largest possible area of Germany before the arrival of the Russians. Thus it would have been judicious for the American commander to have pushed rapidly East in order to be the first to seize Berlin. But Eisenhower did not do this. He kept to the military plan which had been drawn up for the destruction of Germany and its occupation in collaboration with the Red Army, and so he stopped at the Elbe. Thus the Russians were enabled to take Berlin and conquer whatever they could of eastern Germany. Perhaps this policy had been dictated by Washington, but he did not understand how radically the world situation was to be transformed from this moment. Accordingly, I consider that this decision by the Americans was wrong, and I have not changed my opinion today.

"After the Potsdam Conference, an American Colonel told Count Schwerin-Krosigk that it was a matter of indifference to him whether the whole of Germany was occupied by the Russians, and this indeed was the attitude of all American opinion.

"If I had accepted the conditions brought back by General Kinzel on that morning of 6th May, I would have had to hand over our armies in the East to the Russians immediately. I could not accept this, the troops would not have obeyed the order. A mad rout towards the West would have resulted. Thus Eisenhower's conditions were unacceptable, and all I could do was to try and convince him that I could not possibly allow our soldiers and civilians to fall into the hands of the Soviets, and accordingly I had to be content with offering this partial capitulation.

"I summoned Jodl to send him to Friedeburg's help with new instructions. I wrote out a note to Jodl, giving him full power to sign a general capitulation on all fronts, but he was only to use it if he was unable to obtain the first objective, which was a partial capitulation, and then only after he had informed me of the conditions and received my express agreement by cable. On 6th May he flew to Reims.

"On the night of 6th to 7th May I received the following message from him : 'General Eisenhower insists that we must sign now today. Otherwise the Allied lines will be closed against even individual persons who seek to hand themselves over, and all negotiations will be broken off. As I see it, either there is chaos or we sign. Confirm immediately by wireless that I have in fact got full powers to sign the capitulation. Then it can have effect. Hostilities will end on 9th May at o hours, German summer time. Jodl.'

"Eisenhower, we learnt, had again refused any partial capitulation and categorically rejected the two proposals. He told Jodl that he would fire on any German soldier, even unarmed, who approached the American lines in order to surrender himself. However, owing, it would seem, to the more understanding attitude of General Bedell Smith, his Chief of Staff, and to Jodl's statement that in the present condition of our communications, we would need at least two days to get the capitulation order transmitted to all the troops, he finally agreed to a delay of 48 hours, on condition that we signed on the spot. Thus I had to take an immediate decision. According to the telegram, if we signed on the 7th, the troops would still be able to move until o hours on the 9th.

"I was afraid that this delay would not suffice to save either all the soldiers or all the civilians. On the other hand, Jodl had succeeded in obtaining it, and it would nevertheless allow a considerable number of people to regain the security of the West. I would not have gained any advantage by refusing Eisenhower's demand, which would only have produced the chaos which we feared, and the immense and useless loss of human life.

"Consequently, at one o'clock in the morning, I telegraphed to Jodl that he was qualified to sign the general capitulation on this basis, which he did, at Reims, at 2.41 a.m.

"On May 8th, obviously at the wish of the Russians, this formality was repeated at the Headquarters of Marshal Joukov, the Soviet Commander in Chief, at Berlin-Karlshorst. Marshal Keitel, General Stumpff and Admiral Friedeburg signed for the three armed forces. The Western Allies and the Soviets had asked for full powers, which I had expanded, enabling them to carry out this gesture, and these powers were very carefully verified before the ceremony.

"The fate of the soldiers in the East and of the refugees was decided that day. The vast majority of the men in the Southern armies under General Rendulic succeeded in crossing the American demarcation lines. Those under General Lohr in the South Eastern group had less luck. On 9th May a good number of them were still several days march away. Lohr endeavoured by negotiations with the Yugoslavs to lessen the severity of their lot in every possible way, but several tens of thousands nevertheless died in the Yugoslav camps.

"In the North, the American General Carvin, who had occupied part of Mecklenburg on 2nd May with his airborne division, and who was working in with the British advance on Lubeck, since his division was part of the British army, allowed the remains of the 'Vistula Army' to cross behind his lines, but owing to delays numbers of columns of refugees fell into the hands of the Russians, who were following close behind.

"On the centre front, the twelfth army, commanded by General Wenck, had been ordered to free Berlin by attacking towards the East. Wenck succeeded in reaching the region of Potsdam, and thereby opened the road West to the defenders of this town and to the 9th army (General Busse), who brought with them a mass of refugees. But the civilians were not allowed to cross the Elbe. Wenck's army did everything in its power to smuggle over the largest possible number of refugees with them, unknown to the Americans, but this inhuman order condemned a large number of these unfortunates—some of whom had been fleeing for weeks —to the mercy of the Soviets.

"The soldiers of Schoerner's army met an even more deplorable fate. The vast majority of them reached the American lines, but they were not allowed to cross them. They were even fired upon in order to keep them back. After they had so valiantly accomplished their duty, those who did not die of hunger or cold had to endure the rigours of Russian captivity for many long years."

(Grand Admiral Doenitz: *Ten Years and Twenty Days*, translated from the French)

"Obviously", Eisenhower was to write in his *Memoirs*, "the Germans sought to gain time in order to bring back into and behind our lines the maximum number of men who were still fighting in the East. I began to have had enough. I ordered Bedell Smith to tell Jodl that if he did not immediately stop dragging out the negotiations, we would go so far as to use force in order to prevent the refugees from crossing."

(translated from the French)

This in fact is just what the Americans did.

Thus by his obstinate intransigence, Eisenhower handed over hundreds of thousands, and perhaps even millions, of innocent Germans to the appalling bolshevic tyranny which, for the majority, meant either death or the concentration camps and, for the women, the prospect of certain violation. Was he ignorant or unaware of the lot that awaited them? Did he deliberately condemn these unhappy people to this terrible fate in order to carry out the dire Yalta Agreement? That is a question which I cannot answer, but this inhuman order will leave an indelible blot on Eisenhower's memory.

Between 5th May, the date of the armistice concluded with the British, and 9th May, the date of the general capitulation, Admiral Doenitz, by means of all the resources at his disposal, succeeded in rescuing three million German soldiers and civilians, who thus escaped Russian slavery owing to the understanding of Field-Marshal Montgomery.

Postscript

On 12th January 1971, *Le Monde* published (p. 5) a news report concerning the war in Indochina from which we have taken the following extracts:

"The trial of Lieutenant William Calley, the leading defendant accused of the Song-My massacre on 16th March 1968, when several hundred Vietnamese villagers were killed by American troops, reopened yesterday before the court martial at Fort Benning, Georgia. In his memoirs, which he has just published, Lieutenant Calley has implicated the whole American army in Vietnam. For his part, the former public prosecutor of the United States at the Nuremberg War Crimes Trials, Mr. Telford Taylor, considers that the former Commander in Chief of the American forces, General Westmoreland, was just as responsible during the Second World War as his Japanese counterpart was held to be.

" 'If the criteria which were applied against General Yamashita (who was found guilty of atrocities committed by his troops in the Philippines during the Second World War), were likewise applied to army personnel such as General Westmoreland', Mr. Taylor declared, 'he could find himself in the same situation. A general should control the conduct of his troops, and he should be held responsible for it.'

"Today Professor of Law at the University of Columbia, Mr. Taylor is not generally known as a radical. But he considers that the trial by court martial of a lieutenant, a captain and a sergeant for the massacre of the villagers of Song-My is a waste of time, since 'it is not at this level that the really guilty parties will be found'. Besides, he added, 'much more serious' than Song-My was the question of the deaths of all the civilians caused by the bombing raids, and the fact that the peasants were being forced to evacuate their villages. He claims that a Presidential Commission should be set up to investigate war crimes.

"For his part, Lieutenant Calley has stated, both in a declaration to Associated Press and in the memoirs which he has just published, that his trial completely ignored the realities of the war and of what actually happened at Song-My. 'We went to Vietnam to save those people, but we didn't even give them the crumbs off our own table. We hadn't even got the courtesy to learn their language or their customs. We despised them and we killed them.'

"The trial of another member of the company opened before a court martial at Fort MacPherson. A twenty-two-year-old sergeant was accused of having killed half a dozen Vietnam civilians. The young sergeant had admitted, in a statement to the enquiry board on 17th November 1969, that he had taken part in the massacre, and this statement was read out in front of the court martial.

"The soldiers entered the village on 16th March, and it was a massacre, said Sergeant Hutto. We shot into the houses and at people whether stationary or running. I did not agree with these murders, but those were our orders.

"—Can you explain why all the villagers were killed? the prosecutor asked.

"—They were all regarded as Communists, according to Captain Medina.

"—Even the babies and the little children?

"—Yes.

"Towards the end of the cross-examination, Sergeant Hutto's lawyer, Mr. E. Magill, a civilian, asked for an acquittal on the grounds of insufficient evidence. Mr. Magill declared that the responsibility for the massacre lay with Captain Medina, the company commander, and with the other officers who commanded the troops. 'Their duty was to kill', and the soldiers who did so had never been told 'what an illegal order was, or when it is lawful to obey and when it is lawful to disobey', and the lawyer emphasized that his client was not very well educated.

"The Army is holding an enquiry into Captain Medina's activities, but he has not been officially charged, although he has often come under suspicion."

It is obvious that nothing will come of Mr. Taylor's demand for a war crimes commission, but it is equally certain that such a step should be taken if the Nuremberg Trials are to have any moral value at all and be known as something other than the instrument of the victors' vengeance over their defeated enemies.

General Yamashita, who won renown for his lightning victory over the British army at Singapore, was charged at Tokyo as a war criminal, and with the responsibility for the excesses committed by isolated Japanese units who were lost in the depths of the Philippines, and with whom he had had no means of contact. He was condemned to death and hanged. The Japanese, it is true, often behaved with appalling cruelty in the last war, but to pick out General Yamashita as a criminal was a particularly unfortunate choice, since he was a great and honourable soldier, and the suspicion could be laid against the victors that they were avenging their defeat at Singapore.

Furthermore, the legal processes established at Nuremberg served as the basis for a great number of purge trials which were held in France after General de Gaulle came to power, and they created an atmosphere of terror and revolution. As at Nuremberg, obedience to a superior's orders was not considered as an excuse but a crime. The case of General Dentz is a typical example. He was condemned to death for obedience to the orders of a superior, and died in prison from maltreatment.

In these circumstances, I am astonished that no lawyer has used the precedents created at Nuremberg and Paris in 1945, to defend the French officers of the Algerian army, who claimed that obedience to orders from Paris was incompatible with their sense of military honour and their conscience as soldiers.

V

THE MYSTERIOUS TEHERAN AND YALTA AGREEMENTS AND THE SECRET ZABROUSKY DOCUMENT

In 1949 the Spanish Ambassador to Chile, Señor J. M. Doussina-gue, published a book entitled *España Tenia Razon* (Spain Was Right; all the quotations up to p. 86 in this chapter are taken from this book), in which he reveals Spain's attitude towards Soviet communism, the Axis powers and the Allies during the course of the Second World War. At that time he was the principal private secretary of Count Jordana, who was then Spain's Foreign Minister. Thus he was directly involved in the events which he describes in his book at first hand, and he reveals to us a secret document of the utmost importance concerning the Yalta Agreements:

"On 16th April 1943 a sumptuous ceremony was held at Barcelona in the Palace of the Kings of Aragon in honour of the four hundred and fiftieth anniversary of Christopher Columbus' return from his first voyage, when he had been presented to Ferdinand and Isabella and announced the discovery of the New World.

"It was attended by many eminent Spanish and South American personalities. After a solemn Te Deum had been sung in the cathedral of Barcelona, various speeches were delivered in the Royal Palace, including one by the Minister of Foreign Affairs, Count Jordana. Minutely prepared and thought out, his remarks were addressed to the whole world, and should have had considerable repercussions. He announced that Spain was taking a new step forward in pursuance of plan D, which had been drawn up in order to facilitate peace negotiations.

"After asserting Spain's total independence from any foreign influence, he recalled that Spanish policy, in the present as in the past, was based upon Christian principles and traditions, and that in consequence his country could not be identified with those whose regimes were opposed to this ideology, which clearly meant that Spain and her government could not be identified with a political system such as national-socialism."

Set apart from the world conflict, Spain's high mission, at the opportune moment, was to facilitate the re-establishment of a just and fraternal peace, but also to draw the attention of all peoples to the profound spiritual subversion and economic upheavals which would result from the war.

"More terrible and more destructive than the war", said Count Jordana, "more charged with hatred and wicked passions is the Communist revolution which represented all the greater danger since the enormous cost of the war would compromise the social stability of the nations."

Some hours after Count Jordana's speech, Mr. Cordell Hull, American Secretary of State, proclaimed: "The whole world knows that the sole objective of the United Nations is nothing less than the unconditional surrender of Germany."

At that moment Mr. Cordell Hull had only read several telegraphic references to Count Jordana's speech, and not the complete text, and he told the press that he knew nothing about Spain's proposition to negotiate world peace at the earliest possible opportunity.

For their part, Berlin and Rome ignored the proposition, and reaffirmed their determination unhesitatingly to pursue the common struggle until the peril which threatened Europe in both East and West had been overcome.

However, Count Jordana's speech was all the more important since the Spanish government had just been made aware of the existence of a document which was so important that it threatened the security of a great number of European countries. The document in question was a secret letter which had been written by President Roosevelt on 20th February 1943 to the Jew Zabrousky, who was at that time acting as a liaison officer between himself and Stalin.

Here is the full text of this letter:

> The White House, Washington,
> 20th February 1943
>
> Dear Mr. Zabrousky,
>
> As I have already had the pleasure of telling you, together with Mr. Weiss, I am deeply moved to hear that the National Council of Young Israel has been so extremely kind as to propose me as mediator with our common friend Stalin in these difficult moments,

when any menace of friction among the United Nations—in spite of the many self-denying declarations which have been obtained —would have fatal consequences for all, but principally for the USSR itself.

It is therefore in your interest and ours to round off the corners —which becomes difficult to bring about with Litvinoff, to whom I have had, very regretfully, to point out that 'those who sought a quarrel with Uncle Sam would get something to complain about', with regard to internal as well as external affairs. For, having regard to Communist activities in the States of the American Union, his claims are absolutely intolerable.

Timoshenko proved more reasonable in his brief but fruitful visit, and indicated that a new interview with Marshal Stalin might constitute a rapid means of arriving at a direct exchange of views. I reckon that this is more and more urgent, particularly when one remembers all the good which has resulted from Churchill's talk with Stalin.

The United States and Great Britain are ready, without any reservations, to give the USSR absolute parity and voting rights in the future reorganization of the post-war world. She will there-fore take part (as the English Prime Minister let him know when sending him the first draft from Aden) in the directing group in the heart of the Councils of Europe and of Asia; she has a right to this, not only through her vast intercontinental situation, but above all because of her magnificent struggle against Nazism which will win the praise of History and Civilization.

It is our intention—I speak on behalf of our great country and of the mighty British Empire—that these continental councils be constituted by the whole of the independent States in each case, with equitable proportional representation.

And you can, my dear Mr. Zabrousky, assure Stalin that the USSR will find herself on a footing of complete equality, having an equal voice with the United States and England in the direction of the said Councils (of Europe and Asia). Equally with England and the United States, she will be a member of the High Tribunal which will be created to resolve differences between the nations, and she will take part similarly and identically in the selection, preparation, armament and command of the international forces which, under the orders of the Continental Council, will keep watch within each State to see that peace is maintained in the spirit worthy of the League of Nations. Thus these inter-State entities and their associated armies will be able to impose their decisions and to make themselves obeyed.

This being the case, a position so elevated in the Tetrarchy of the Universe ought to give Stalin enough satisfaction not to renew claims which are capable of creating insoluble problems for us. In this way, the American continent will remain outside all Soviet influence and within the exclusive concern of the United States, as we have promised the countries of our continent it shall.

In Europe, France will gravitate into the British orbit. We have reserved for France a secretariat with a consultative voice but without voting rights, as a reward for her present resistance and as a penalty for her former weakness.

Portugal, Spain, Italy and Greece will develop under the protection of England towards a modern civilization which will lift them out of their historical decline.

We will grant the USSR an access to the Mediterranean; we will accede to her wishes concerning Finland and the Baltic, and we shall require Poland to show a judicious attitude of comprehension and compromise; Stalin will still have a wide field for expansion in the little, unenlightened countries of Eastern Europe —always taking into account the rights which are due to the fidelity of Yugoslavia and Czecho-Slovakia—he will completely recover the territories which have temporarily been snatched from Great Russia.

Most important of all: after the partition of the Third Reich and the incorporation of its fragments with other territories to form new nationalities which will have no link with the past, the German threat will conclusively disappear in so far as being any danger to the USSR, to Europe and the entire world.

Turkey—but it will serve no useful purpose to discuss that question further, it needs full understanding, and Churchill has given the necessary assurances to President Inonu, in the name of us both. The access to the Mediterranean contrived for Stalin ought to content him.

Asia—we are in agreement with his demands, except for any complications which may arise later. As for Africa—again what need for discussion? We must give something back to France and even compensate her for her losses in Asia. It will also be necessary to give Egypt something, as has already been promised to the Wafdist government. As regards Spain and Portugal, they will have to be recompensed for the renunciations necessary to achieve better universal balance. The United States will also share in the distribution by right of conquest and they will be obliged to claim some points which are vital for their zone of influence; that is only fair. Brazil, too, must be given the small colonial expansion which has been offered to her.

In view of the rapid annihilation of the Reich, convince Stalin—my dear Mr. Zabrousky—that he ought to give way, for the good of all, in the matter of the colonies in Africa, and to abandon all propaganda and intervention in the industrial centres of America. Assure him also of my complete understanding and of my entire sympathy and desire to facilitate these solutions, which makes more timely than ever the personal discussion which I propose—the above is only a general outline of a plan which is intended for further study.

This is the issue and the whole issue.

As I told you at the time, I was very pleased at the gracious terms of the letter informing me of your decision and of the desire you expressed to offer me in the name of the National Council a copy of the greatest treasure of Israel, the scroll of the Torah. This letter will convey the confirmation of my acceptance; to those who are so frank with me, I respond with the greatest confidence. Be so good, I beg of you, to transmit my gratitude to the distinguished body over which you preside, recalling the happy occasion of the banquet on its 31st anniversary.

I wish you every success in your work as interpreter.

Very sincerely yours,
(signed) Franklin Roosevelt.

This version of the letter has been translated from the French, which in turn was taken from the original Spanish as published on pages 198–199 of Señor Doussinague's book, *España Tenia Razon*, and the author commented upon it as follows:

"So, by the benevolent resolve of Mr. Roosevelt, who was then preparing for the Teheran Conference in full agreement with Stalin, Central Europe, with the exception of Turkey and Greece —though the latter was to be deprived of Thrace in order to give the USSR free access to the Mediterranean—the Baltic countries, and certain countries of Western Europe such as Holland, Belgium and Switzerland, were to come under Soviet domination; Germany was to be dismembered; while the Asiatic continent, including the French colonies, would also enter the Soviet sphere. In Africa certain promises were made to Stalin. As the counterpart to this, in Western Europe, Italy, France, Spain and Portugal were to pass under the protection of England. America would remain entirely outside the influence and propaganda of the Soviets.

"But what is more, the USSR would take a hand in the choice

and preparation of international forces which were to be active within all European States, including those of the West; and the Asian States, constituted as the Council of Asia, and the European States, constituted as the Council of Europe, were to be directed by a group comprising the United States, the USSR, England and China, on a footing of complete equality, in complete disregard to the right to independence possessed by each of the countries so disposed of, and also of all that was representative of Christian civilization in the Continent of Europe.

"Spain, together with all the other European countries, would be subject to this directory body of which her worst enemy would be a member—the same enemy which had led the fight against us throughout the Civil War, and which could never forgive Spain for the defeat that had been inflicted on it under the guidance of Franco.

"A mere glance at this letter is enough to explain the amazement, the agitation and the fear we felt when we became aware of it. Our ardent desire to see peace come with all speed, before President Roosevelt's plans could be realized, can easily be imagined. Knowledge of this letter was the key to all the actions and gestures of Spain and served as a basis for the political discussions of its rulers. Thanks to this letter *we knew* (Doussinague's italics) what to expect of the post-war period . . . an immense catastrophe threatened to descend on Europe and on all its old civilization."

One month later, on 9th May 1943, General Franco made an important speech at Almeira from which we have extracted the principal passages:

"After he had renewed Spain's appeal for peace, since he considered it was madness to continue a war behind which there loomed up the spectre of something infinitely worse, General Franco explained how communism, the sower of hatred and barbarism, represented the image of the anti-Europe, the negation of our civilization and the destruction of everything which we hold most dear and valuable.

"In making this speech, General Franco had in mind Roosevelt's letter to Zabrousky, and he hoped that a solution would be found to end the conflict before the incredible concessions which the letter promised to Russia were carried out.

"One of the principal obstacles which would confront the Spanish plan for peace was the existence of a real incompatibility between national socialist ideals and those of the rest of the civilized world. If the Spanish proposition was to have a chance of succeeding, it would be necessary to diminish the gap between these principles, which were not only political, but even more of a religious nature.

"Two days after this speech, the United States Ambassador, Mr. Carlton Hayes, sent a secret letter to the State Department in Washington, whose contents became known to the Spanish government, in which he requested that the Barcelona and Almeira statements should not be interpreted in the United States as being inspired by the Axis. Spain, he wrote, seeks above all to preserve an independent policy which is not subject to any foreign power, she wishes to avoid any compromise, and she has decided to fight any aggressor from whatever side an attack might be mounted against her, either by the Axis or the Allies. Nevertheless it is true that she is in favour of victory going to the Allies.

'The Spanish plan D for peace was met with scepticism on both sides of the struggle. A furious press campaign was let loose against Spain, especially after the Barcelona and Almeira statements, in England but above all in America, where the war was not popular and the government had been compelled to conduct an active propaganda campaign to convince the people of the necessity of the war.

"Roosevelt, who had a wrong impression of Spain, had drawn up a plan for the invasion of Spain at the same time that American troops were disembarking in Africa, and he also set off a slanderous press and radio campaign in order to prepare public opinion for this eventuality. However the conciliatory attitude of the Spanish government and the assurance that no measure would be taken prejudicial to the Allies and their future military operations in the Mediterranean were recognized by the United States Ambassador in Madrid, who wrote to the State Department on 22nd June 1943 to this effect.

"Towards the end of 1942 and in the early part of 1943 the Allies brought increasing pressure to bear on Spain to improve her relations with the Soviet Republic. At that time Russia had begun to take the initiative in the attack, and began a series of victories which were to lead her from the Volga to Berlin. She was held in considerable prestige by the Allies, who were then of the opinion that communism was less dangerous to the economic life of a country than Nazism.

"But for Spain, on the contrary, Russia was still the real, common enemy of England and the United States, as well as of Germany and Italy. This opinion was strongly contested by

America, who invited Spain to collaborate with Russia unless she wished to lose her economic aid from the United States.

"Spanish ambassadors had an exchange of views on this subject with the governments of Germany and Italy, as well as with the Vatican.

"On 18th March 1943 His Holiness Pope Pius XII received our ambassador, M. Barcenas, in audience. He congratulated him on the agreement which existed between the Spanish government and the Vatican, and approved our attitude with regard to the menace of national-socialism. On the latter subject he had some very hard words to say, and he was under no illusion that in time there would come a lessening of the anti-religious policy of the Reich.

"It was during this period of tension that on 21st October 1943 Mr. Hayes, the United States Ambassador at Madrid, sent Count Jordana a letter in which he spoke in the name of his government. He blamed Spain for confusing communism with Russia, and requested him to cease making official attacks against the latter country which was an important member of the United Nations and an ally of the United States. The American Ambassador accused the Spanish government of complacency towards Nazi Germany and of being thus the only free country to favour the latter. 'Communism,' he wrote, 'was essentially an interior problem of Russia's and in no way affected any country whose standard of living was sufficiently high to render its development impossible.' According to Hayes, Spain's systematic attacks against Soviet Russia would make it difficult for the Allies to continue their economic aid to Spain, for not only had they no intention whatever of opposing communism at the end of the war, but they were going to permit Russia to collaborate closely with the United Nations in future international peace conferences.

"Briefly, the United States were displeased with Spain's attitude to Russia and felt that it constituted a powerful obstacle preventing the amelioration of their mutual relations. Finally, the American Ambassador left Count Jordana with a note resuming the tenor of his communication. When he had departed, Count Jordana read the note with care and wrote at the head of the first page: 'This note is of the utmost gravity since it is not written in his own name but in the name of his government.'

"A few days later Count Jordana replied to the American Ambassador. Distinguishing between the American point of view, which was influenced by the psychology of the war and by the powerful aid which Russia contributed towards a common victory, Count Jordana showed that the real problem lay on a spiritual level which far surpassed the actual development of events. The war was in fact a passing phenomenon and only secondary to the heart of the problem, which lay in communism.

"Spain, from its privileged situation as a neutral country, was in a position to study the grave problems of the day with greater serenity and objectivity, and because her policy was founded on Christian principles she considered that the most fundamental problem of the age lay in the bolshevic revolutionary movement of the masses who had been robbed of their faith, and which tended to seize countries by means of disorder and violence."

Here are the principal passages from Count Jordana's letter:

"As General Franco has on many an occasion stated, and in particular in his speech on 1st October, Spain considers that independently of the outcome of the war, and behind it, the world is faced with a spiritual problem of the utmost importance created by the revolutionary conditions of masses who have been separated from all belief in God, and whose aim is to improve their economic situation by recourse to violence and the utterly unscrupulous use of any means whatever. This revolutionary spirit, which is comprised of varying hues, is known by the generic name of bolshevism. The war is only a passing phenomenon as long as this spirit, which is much deeper and more lasting than the war itself, exists.

"I am sure Your Excellency will understand my astonishment and apprehension at learning that it is your conviction that the revolutionary peril can be overcome simply by raising the standard of living of the needy classes, as if there were not millions of communist party members in the most economically advanced countries. I can hardly believe that someone could imagine that this gigantic peril which threatens our civilization can be resolved by the mere adjustment of salaries. No, Your Excellency, it is not only an economic question, nor even a social problem in the widest sense of the word . . . we are confronted with a spiritual problem, an evil of the utmost gravity which reaches down to the deepest levels in the human soul, for when you teach the masses that morality is only a bourgeois prejudice and that there is no superior justice to which we are responsible for our acts, you remove the brake and urge them to attack any obstacle which opposes the satisfaction of their most brutal instincts. . . .

"One cannot state that bolshevism is simply an internal problem of the Russians. The Spanish government is in possession of documents and proofs which demonstrate that the Spanish communist movement was organized by agents who came from Moscow; and nobody can be ignorant of the fact that the revolutionary spirit which bubbles up from underground throughout the whole world is internally upheld and supported by the government of the Soviet Union. Its slogan, 'Proletarians of the world, unite' is the flag of rebellion against our present society and an appeal to its destruction.

"The Soviet Union advocates the dictatorship of the proletariat, a regime which is to be imposed by force. While Spain has no quarrel with the Russian nation as such, she is extremely uneasy at contemplating the self-proclaimed mission of the Soviet Union to foment revolution throughout the entire world . . . and at the hands of which she has suffered so much in recent years herself, with the blood of thousands of deaths and enormous destruction of property caused by communist activity in her own country.

"When one considers the real image of the Soviet Union, and its doctrine and sombre designs, it was not without apprehension that Spain witnessed the military victories of the Soviets, behind which there reared up the spectacle of a terrifying future, notably for those European countries occupied by the Soviet armies. This is why Spain could not share the optimism of the United States Ambassador, neither as far as concerned the so-called religious liberty said to exist in the Soviet Union at the present time, and which in the final analysis would appear to be a purely political expedient, nor as far as concerns a supposed evolution of the Soviet regime.

"Spain can state with a full realization of the truth of the assertion that any democratic regime which in any way resembled the Soviet system would be abused by Russian agents who benefiting from the liberty conferred on them by the former, would use it to work for their own ends and for the eventual substitution of their own regime. This is precisely what happened at Madrid during the Civil War when Largo Caballero, 'the Spanish Lenin' and the head of the red government, was overthrown by a republican-democratic faction which sprang from the communist bloc. Although the republicans themselves had tolerated communist atrocities without protest, they were nevertheless driven out in their turn by the Russian agents and their henchmen who stirred up a veritable revolution with violent strife in March 1939."

Señor Doussinague continues:

"The Spanish Foreign Minister had received the very clear impression that the exchange which had been begun by Ambassador Hayes had expressed the point of view of the State Department, and his reply of 29th October, which set out with great sincerity and solid argumentation the doctrinal basis of Spanish thinking and policy towards the war, was the most important statement of its kind yet to have been published.

"Ambassador Hayes' reply to the Spanish Foreign Minister, dated 27th December 1943, took some little notice of the arguments presented by Count Jordana, but neverthless considered that Russia was a victim of German aggression."

We have extracted the principal points of this reply below:

"The Ambassador agreed that communist Marxism was a real danger for the free world, but at the same time he thought that Spain, under the influence of the recent civil war, had an exaggerated fear of Russia and an immoderate confidence in Nazi Germany.

"He could not believe that Russian communism, despite the regime of terror with which it had been inaugurated and its subversive influence in Spain before and during the civil war, constituted a greater danger than German nazism, which he held represented a much greater threat to the liberty of the nations and to traditional, Christian civilization. It was Germany which had attacked Russia and Europe, in order to devastate them. The American Ambassador forgot that in 1939, by agreement with Germany, Soviet Russia had invaded Poland, Lithuania, Estonia and Latvia, all of whose inhabitants had been deported, and had brutally attacked Finland.

"After the war, he thought, the Russian menace to Europe and the world would in no way compare to the threat posed by the alliance between Nazi Germany and pagan Japan. Besides, for a long time Russia would be dependent on her allies for aid to enable her to repair her own ravages and for that reason alone would be obliged to observe the Atlantic Charter. The rebirth of religious feeling and patriotism was a guarantee of her goodwill and desire for international collaboration. Therefore Spain could no longer continue in the role of peacemaker if she still persisted in an intransigent attitude to Russia.

"On 11th January 1944 Count Jordana replied to Hayes and told him that the struggle in which Spain was engaged against communism was far superior in concept to that being waged by the Axis. It was always necessary to distinguish between the errors of Hitler's regime, which were repugnant to the catholic conscience of the Spanish nation, and Germany's geographical situation in the front line of the defence of Europe against the appalling storm arising in the steppes of Asia. A call for the rectification of the equivocal doctrines of nazism was no reason for destroying the defensive strength of Germany considered as a front line of resistance against the deadly invasion from Asia, and for that reason it was essential to save Germany from the risk of annihilation. To put it briefly, if nazism was a decidedly abominable idea, for a diplomat Germany represented a European reality which had to be taken into consideration.

"The American Ambassador and his collaborators nevertheless continued to work for an improvement in the relations between Spain and the United States, after the correspondence terminated, but they had little illusion that they would succeed in changing the opinion of Count Jordana and the Spanish government.

"In December the Teheran conference took place, and two men, Stalin and Roosevelt, whom Churchill attempted in vain to oppose, disposed of the fate of the whole world without being subject to any control whatever, and freely shuffled the cards determining the future of non-communist countries and the lot of their inhabitants.

"We know now," Señor Doussinague wrote, "that for military reasons Eisenhower and the American government opposed Churchill's plan envisaging a landing in the Balkans. If Churchill's plan had been accepted, the history of these latter years would not have been quite so filled with tears and horror.

"In general, the strictly military outlook concentrates its efforts on solving the problems immediately to hand. Thus it sacrifices the future, or, which comes back to the same thing, it prepares new problems which are sometimes even more grave than they would have been had they not been foreseen and stifled before taking shape. The real statesman is the man who can stand up in a high observation post and command a long view. If you abandon criteria of policy during the struggle, you close your eyes to the morrow."

It now remains to bring this chapter of Spanish history to its conclusion.

Roosevelt's secret letter to Zabrousky, published in Señor Doussinague's book, is an extremely important document, and it seems quite extraordinary that such a document, reproduced in a book of an official character which had been written by a diplomat who was formerly Count Jordana's secretary, and placed publicly on sale in Madrid—it seems extraordinary, I maintain, that this document should have remained practically unknown outside Spain. As far as I am aware, it has only been mentioned in a French newspaper some years ago, but the journalist who wrote the article about it does not seem to have understood its importance, and its publication produced practically no reaction at all. The United States Embassy, when consulted about the document, was manifestly extremely embarrassed, and delayed a long time before finally sending a brief note in reply saying that the State Department had found no trace of the letter in its archives.

Quite apart from the inherent prudence of all diplomatic service, this reply really carries no significance since it is a question of a personal and secret exchange of correspondence between President Roosevelt and Mr. Zabrousky, his intermediary with Stalin.

The Spanish Government has not divulged its source, nor, in its place, would any other government have done so. All we know is that it was a feminine personality in the immediate circle around Roosevelt who secretly communicated the document to the Spanish Government.

The Spanish Government was absolutely certain of its authenticity since their policy and the speeches of their rulers have been profoundly influenced by it; furthermore, it is an undeniable fact that the agreements reached at Teheran and Yalta were in conformity with the lines indicated in this famous letter.

I have personally questioned the author of the book, Señor Doussinague, who granted me an interview when he was Ambassador at Rome. Naturally he did not reveal any diplomatic secrets, but he made the following very judicious remarks:

"The authenticity of the document is apparent merely from its context. Carry yourself back to the time with which it deals; who was there among us—unless it were some prophet, who would have been accused of being out of his mind—who could have imagined in advance that Roosevelt, acting in his personal capacity, was about to hand over half of Europe and Asia to the Soviets, secretly and without gaining anything in return?"

Finally, a certain number of conclusions may be drawn from this document.

1. There have been attempts to excuse Roosevelt on the score that at Yalta he was a dying man unable to defend himself in the conduct of the negotiations. The letter to Zabrousky, on the con-

trary, proves that the Yalta Agreement had been prepared far in advance by a secret understanding between Roosevelt and Stalin.

2. It was Jews who served as intermediaries between Roosevelt and Stalin, confirming the enormous influence which Jewish advisers of his immediate circle exerted over Roosevelt, and their Communist tendencies.

3. Jewish circles therefore bear a heavy responsibility for the disastrous Treaty of Yalta and for the seizures made by the Soviets in Europe and Asia.

4. This does not relieve Roosevelt in any way of his personal responsibility. His lack of awareness of what he was doing and his failure to comprehend Stalin's communism remain utterly amazing. There are only two possible explanations for his attitude : either he was truly ignorant, to an astonishing degree for a politician who was so astute, or he was a conscious agent of subversion, entirely dominated by the Jewish influences around him.

In either event, his presence at the head of the American Government, and the latter's omnipotence, at a crucial moment in history, represented a very grave danger which threatened the future of the whole world and in particular of western civilization. America, however, was the first to suffer the effects of this disastrous policy, which was so blind to reality, and today Count Jordana's predictions have indeed come true.

For many years now, America has been engaged in a cold war with Russian and Chinese communism, and maintains a gigantic strength of naval, military and air defences which are kept in a state of permanent alert in readiness for the outbreak of war.

She has replaced Germany in an "unholy alliance with pagan Japan"; she waged a costly war against Chinese communism in Korea, and in South East Asia is still conducting a bloody struggle against the Viet Cong, who are supported by Russian and Chinese communism, and which she is far from winning; not to mention, Cuba, South America, Africa and other hot spots throughout the globe.

As time goes on and the light of history becomes clearer, we can reaffirm with greater certitude : yes, Spain was right.

*   *   *

The tragic events in Czecho-Slovakia have focused attention anew on the Yalta Agreement. The United States have been accused of doing nothing to oppose the invasion of Czecho-Slovakia by Russian tanks, because this country came under the zone of influence attributed to the Russians in Europe by the Yalta Agreement.

In reply to this charge, the United States special envoy in Paris, Mr. Averell Harriman, who was leading negotiations with Vietnam, recently stated with great firmness that no division of the world into zones of influence took place at Yalta.

The Zabrousky document, which we have published, shows that at least in Roosevelt's mind such a division took place. But the Zabrousky letter is a secret document whose authenticity can only be proved by the Spanish Government, although it is true that Count Jordana, who was then Spanish Foreign Minister, had no doubt whatever as to its validity.

However, when my *Freemasonry and the Vatican*, in which an English version of the Zabrousky letter was published for the first time (pp. 182–184), was launched in London in the spring of 1968, I held a press conference at which I was approached by an American member of the audience, who told me that the document is unquestionably authentic, since confirmation of it may be found in the Memoirs of Cardinal Spellman. Researching this clue, I found that there is in fact a long passage in these memoirs which constitutes an implicit and very striking confirmation of this famous document.

On 2nd September 1943, the Cardinal, who was then Archbishop Spellman, dined at the White House with President Roosevelt and Winston Churchill, and on the following morning he had a long conversation, lasting an hour and a half, entirely alone with the President, and which he wrote down at once in his memoirs. In it the Cardinal resumes Roosevelt's thoughts as he had expounded them in the course of the interview, and here they are as related by Rev. R. I. Gannon, SJ, in *The Cardinal Spellman Story*:

"It is planned to make an agreement among the Big Four. Accordingly the world will be divided into spheres of influence: China gets the Far East; the US the Pacific; Britain and Russia, Europe and Africa. But as Britain has predominantly colonial interests it might be assumed that Russia will predominate in Europe. Although Chiang Kai-shek will be called in on the great decisions concerning Europe, it is understood that he will have no influence on them. The same thing might become true—although to a lesser degree—for the US. He hoped, 'although it might be wishful thinking,' that the Russian intervention in Europe would not be too harsh.

"*League of Nations:*
"The last one was no success, because the small states were allowed to intervene. The future League will consist only of the four big powers (US, Britain, Russia, China). The small states will

have a consultative assembly, without right to decide or to vote. For example, at the armistice with Italy, the Greeks, Jugoslavs and French asked to be co-signers. 'We simply turned them down.' They have no right to sit in where the big ones are. Only the Russians were admitted, because they are big, strong and simply impose themselves.

"Russia:

"An interview with Stalin will be forced as soon as possible. He believes that he will be better fitted to come to an understanding with Stalin than Churchill. Churchill is too idealistic, he is a realist. So is Stalin. Therefore an understanding between them on a realistic basis is probable. The wish is, although it seems improbable, to get from Stalin a pledge not to extend Russian territory beyond a certain line. He would certainly receive: Finland, the Baltic States, the Eastern half of Poland, Bessarabia. There is no point to oppose these desires of Stalin, because he has the power to get them anyhow. So better give them gracefully.

"Furthermore the population of Eastern Poland wants to become Russian. Still it is absolutely not sure whether Stalin will be satisfied with these boundaries. On the remark that Russia has appointed governments of communistic character for Germany, Austria and other countries which can make a communist regime there, so that the Russians might not even need to come, he agreed that this is to be expected. Asked further, whether the Allies would not do something from their side which might offset this move in giving encouragement to the better elements, just as Russia encourages the Communists, he declared that no such move was contemplated. It is therefore probable that Communist Regimes would expand, but what can we do about it. France might eventually escape, if it has a government à la Leon Blum. The Front Populaire would be so advanced, that eventually the Communists might accept it. On the direct question whether Austria, Hungary and Croatia would fall under some sort of Russian protectorate, the answer was clearly yes. But he added, we should not overlook the magnificent economic achievements of Russia. Their finances are sound. It is natural that the European countries will have to undergo tremendous changes in order to adapt to Russia, but he hopes that in ten or twenty years the European influences would bring the Russians to become less barbarian.

"Be it as it may, he added, the US and Britain cannot fight the Russians. The Russian production is so big that the American help, except for trucks, is negligible. He hopes that out of a forced friendship may soon come a real and lasting friendship. The European people will simply have to endure the Russian domination, in the hope that in ten or twenty years they will be able to live well with the Russians. Finally he hopes, the Russians will get 40% of the Capitalist regime, the capitalists will retain only 60% of their system, and so an understanding will be possible. This is the opinion of Litvinoff.

"Austria:
"No plan for the Austrian Government in Exile is made or tolerated. There will be no opposition to a Russian dominated Communist Austrian Regime. The one thing that would save Austria from the Communists would be if Otto of Austria succeeded to gain that throne with the help of Hungary. But even then he would have to deal with the Russians.

"Germany:
"Agreement has been reached between R[oosevelt] and Churchill, that Germany will be divided into several states. It will have no more central government, but will be under the domination of the Big Four, mostly Russia. There will be no peace treaty, but simply a decree of the Big Four. Before that hearings would be held, but these would have no influence. Germany would be divided into the following states: Bavaria, Rhineland. Saxony, Hesse, Prussia. Württemberg would become part of Bavaria, Saxony would take parts of Prussia. Hanover would become an independent state; Germany would be disarmed for forty years. No air force, no civilian aviation, no German would be authorized to learn flying.

"Poland:
"Poland, if re-established, would get Eastern Prussia.

"Other Countries:
"Plebiscites would be held in the following countries: France, Italy, Netherlands, Belgium, Norway, Greece. No plebiscite is to be expected in Czecho-Slovakia.

"How far this type of 'realism' reflected the thinking of Roosevelt's 'favourite Bishop' can be gathered from the deep concern voiced at this time by the American hierarchy on the increasing influence of Soviet Russia in the distribution of the spoils of war. Its members agreed that secularism, exploitation, and totalitarianism, whether Fascist, Nazi, or Communist, could never lead to a lasting peace, while Archbishop Spellman himself was urging everywhere that we keep the spirit of revenge out of our activities and 'win the war without destroying our victory'.

"While the Archbishop was still a guest in the White House, word came that Montgomery had slipped two divisions across the Straits of Messina and the Allied invasion of the Continent was at last an accomplished fact. The joy of the news with its implication of approaching victory was tempered for many by the increased danger of the Holy Father's situation."

         (R. I. Gannon : *The Cardinal Spellman Story*, pp. 222–225)

"By this time, however, the writer's sincere devotion to the President was already troubled by doubts. The more he thought about the policy of unconditional surrender and discussed it with military authorities of the highest rank, the more impossible it was for him to accept it. He could see that it not only stiffened German resistance and cost both sides innumerable casualties, but it made everything the Pope and he himself had been praying for seem so futile. The Holy Father's favourite phrase, repeated again and again, had been 'Peace with Justice,' but what armed forces had ever been just with an utterly prostrate foe? . . . to complicate matters, the second Conference at Quebec had been held in September. There the plan of Secretary Morgenthau to annihilate the German people by dismembering their country and giving pieces of flesh to all the neighbours; by wrecking all the mines and factories and condemning seventy million human beings to live off a piece of land that would not feed half of them; a plan characterized by Secretary Hull as one of 'blind vengeance,' had been accepted by Churchill and Roosevelt almost without reservation.

"On the same day that Hull had received the President's memo embracing the Morgenthau plan, he received another informing him that Morgenthau had presented at Quebec, in conjunction with the plan for Germany, a proposal of credits to Britain in the amount of six and a half billion dollars. The Secretary of State wrote later : 'This might suggest to some the *quid pro quo* with which the Secretary of the Treasury was able to get Mr. Churchill's adherence to his cataclysmic plan for Germany. . . . This whole development at Quebec, I believe, angered me as much as anything that had happened during my career as Secretary of State.'

"On Roosevelt's return to Washington, Hull found that 'he did not seem to realize the devastating nature of the memorandum of

15th September to which he had put his "O.K.—F.D.R." ' Later in the month, Secretary Stimson had a talk with the President from which he drew the same conclusion :

"He informed me [said Hull] that he had thereupon read to the President several sentences from the President's memorandum of 15th September, concluding with the phrase 'looking forward to converting Germany into a country primarily agricultural and pastoral in its character.'

"Stimson informed me that the President was frankly staggered at hearing these sentences and said that he had no idea how he could have initialled the memorandum, and that he had evidently done so without much thought.

"This ominous change that was coming over the President was not lost on the observant Archbishop. It brought back to his mind snatches of conversation that had disturbed him during the past year in many of their friendly visits together. He could recall the disarming smile with which Roosevelt would say, 'The Pope is too worried about communism,' and the rich tones of his voice as he expressed his sympathy with the great Soviet democracy. 'Russia,' he said one evening when they were sitting around after dinner in the White House, 'has need of protection. She has been invaded twice, you know. That is why we shall give her part of Poland and recompense Poland with a part of Germany.'

"The Archbishop protested, 'But your decision cannot cause a part of Poland to become Russia except by driving the population off their land. It is immoral to uproot people like that and take away their homes and their churches and even their cemeteries.'

"He remembered especially the interview the week before the President left for his conference with Stalin and Churchill at Teheran. It had shocked him profoundly that Roosevelt would go much more than halfway to meet the Red dictator in his own back yard, and he told him so. Nor was he reconciled when his 'old friend' answered with a smile, 'Don't worry. I know how to talk to Stalin. He is just another practical man who wants peace and prosperity.'

"The Archbishop answered, 'He is not just another anything. He is different. You can't trust him. He'll never co-operate.'

"Worried as he often was, however, he would conclude that despite occasional signs of irresponsibility, coupled with loose social and political planning, F.D.R. was still a genius, a very charming genius, and able to end the horrors of a world war."

(R. I. Gannon, ibid., pp. 245–246)

"After a few months, however, as details of the things that
were done at Yalta gradually seeped through to the American
people, the Archbishop's old doubts and fears began to grow into
genuine disillusionment. The climax came when His Excellency
learned that his one-time ideal had handed over to Soviet Russia,
not only Southern Sukhalin but all the Kurile Islands too, for it
stirred the memory of a certain evening at the White House just
after his return from Alaska. It was a painfully vivid memory.
Roosevelt had been summing up for his guests the events in the
Pacific Theatre and pointing to a map on the wall that showed
the Kurile Islands, said dramatically: 'those islands are a dagger
aimed at the heart of America. They must never fall into the
hands of an enemy'. The Archbishop realized, with a sinking
feeling, that the dagger was now in the hands of our most
dangerous enemy and that a sick President had unwittingly put it
there."

(R. I. Gannon, ibid., p. 248)

VI

THE MORGENTHAU, KAUFMAN AND BAR-ZOHAR DOCUMENTS

The Internal Security Subcommittee of the United States Senate Committee on the Judiciary has recently published a series of documents which present very detailed information on the extraordinary activities of the Secretary of the Treasury during the crucial years 1934–1945, Henry Morgenthau, Jr. These documents are of the utmost interest, for they unveil the whole of the secret history of the foreign policy of the American Government during this period.

Entitled *Morgenthau Diary*, and published by the US Government Printing Office in Washington in November 1967, the documents are published in a work which consists of two enormous volumes of a total of some 1,650 pages dealing exclusively with American policy with regard to the war, Germany, and Europe, and they were prepared by the Subcommittee to investigate the administration of the Internal Security Act and other Internal Security Laws of the Committee on the Judiciary.

As the foreword of the publication itself states, "Dr. Anthony Kubek, Professor of History at Dallas University, and head of its History Department, acted as a consultant to the Subcommittee in the selection of the documents and has written an introduction to place events recounted in the diary items in their proper historical perspective. The Kubek analysis is regarded as both brilliantly presented and historically sound, and the Subcommittee is proud to offer these additional portions of the Morgenthau Diaries together with Dr. Kubek's introduction, for the information of the Senate." This analysis is some 81 pages long, and in the following pages I shall give a résumé of Dr. Kubek's findings, quoting extracts from the most important passages.

"The Morgenthau Diaries," Dr. Kubek informs us, "run to 864 numbered volumes, with additional unnumbered volumes, bringing the total to 900. Each contains about 300 pages. In all, there are approximately one million words of transcripts of conversations among high-ranking Treasury officials . . . the documents in the present volume deal primarily with the Treasury Department's policy towards Germany during World War II and in the immediate postwar period. This data not only serves a historical purpose regarding events prior to and during the Second World War, but also indicates the serious problem of a Cabinet department exceeding its jurisdiction by presuming to make foreign policy as a result of unauthorized, uncontrolled and often dangerous power exercised by nonelected officials."

(*Morgenthau Diary*, p. 1)

A footnote at this point states that "Morgenthau himself recognized the potential usefulness of the Diaries. A week after his resignation in July 1945 he discussed with his aides the question of what to do with the Diaries. Assistant Secretary Dan Bell warned that there was material in the Diaries 'embarrassing' to many individuals because 'we have talked quite frankly in your conferences about a lot of people'. Morgenthau's secretary, Mrs. H. Klotz, agreed. The Treasury Attorney, J. Pehle, was worried that the Republicans, if they 'got in' and began 'investigating the Roosevelt regime' might subpoena the Diaries. He advised, therefore, that the Diaries 'be carefully edited and the personal and flippant material deleted'. This, he told Morgenthau, 'would be in your own interest and in the public interest' " (ibid.).

These documents, therefore, published by the Government of the United States, bear an absolutely indisputable stamp of official authenticity, and they reveal the enormous influence which his Jewish advisers—Bernard Baruch, H. Morgenthau Jr., Harry Dexter White and others—exercised on President Roosevelt. At a crucial epoch in the history of the world a group of Jews in political circles succeeded in secretly orientating the foreign policy of the United States, and they played a major role in the development of events in Europe. It is not stating it too strongly to say that it was a question of Secretary of the Treasury Morgenthau, surrounded by exclusively Jewish collaborators and advisers, pursuing a policy which was dictated purely by Jewish concerns and without for one moment caring about American interests.

Profiting from the friendship which existed between himself and President Roosevelt, Morgenthau completely exceeded his position, and although he was really only Secretary of the Treasury, he nevertheless took control of American foreign policy during the years 1934–1945, ignoring the Ministers of War and State Department who were normally the properly qualified men to handle these affairs, but who were powerless to oppose him and who sometimes were quite simply ignorant of decisions which had been taken in secret by Morgenthau and Roosevelt.

A most notable example of this instance was the famous Quebec Conference, where decisions vital to the future of Europe were taken by Roosevelt and Churchill. The only others present were Morgenthau and Harry Dexter White, for Stimson and Hull, the Ministers of War and of the State Department were carefully excluded. How many people remember that the abolition of diplomatic secrecy had been formulated by Wilson in 1918 when President of the USA, as one of the essential bases of democracy?

"Before Morgenthau was appointed Secretary of the Treasury, he had lived near Roosevelt's home at Hyde Park, N.Y., for two decades, and could be counted as one of his closest and most trusted friends."

(*Morgenthau Diary*, p. 2)

It is this friendship which explains his nomination to the Treasury and the enormous influence which he exerted throughout the whole war upon American foreign policy.

"The conduct of American foreign policy today consumes such a large share of the annual budget that the Secretary of the Treasury and his financial experts automatically become involved in diplomatic decisions of all kinds. In Roosevelt's time, however, Secretary Morgenthau's deep involvement in questions of international significance sorely annoyed other Cabinet members and created considerable friction with the State Department. . . . In his *Memoirs* (vol. 1, pp. 207–208) Secretary of State Cordell Hull described it in these terms: 'Emotionally upset by Hitler's rise and his persecution of the Jews, Morgenthau often sought to induce the President to anticipate the State Department or to act contrary to our better judgement. We sometimes found him conducting negotiations with foreign governments which were the function of the State Department. His work in drawing up a catastrophic plan for the post-war treatment of Germany, and inducing the President to accept it without consultation with the State Department, was an outstanding example of this interference.'

"Elsewhere in his *Memoirs* (vol. 1, p. 207) Hull acknowledges that Morgenthau was an able administrator with an 'excellent organisation . . . headed by Harry Dexter White'. Actually it was Dr. Harry Dexter White, Morgenthau's principal adviser on monetary matters and finally Assistant Secretary of the Treasury, who conducted much of the important business of the Department. The Diaries reveal that White's influence was enormous throughout the years of World War II" (ibid., p. 2).

"Shortly after Morgenthau became Secretary in 1934, White joined his staff as an economic analyst on the recommendation of the noted economist, Prof. Jacob Viner of the University of Chicago. . . . In 1938 the position of Director of Monetary Research was created for him, and in the summer of 1941 he was given the additional title and duties of 'Assistant to the Secretary'. Articulate, moustachioed, and nattily dressed, he was a conspicuous figure in the Treasury but remained unknown to the public until 1943, when newspaper articles identified him as the actual architect of Secretary Morgenthau's monetary proposals for the post-war period.

"The Diaries reveal White's technique of domination over general Treasury affairs by submitting his plans and ideas to the Secretary, who frequently carried them directly to the President. It is very significant that Morgenthau had access to the President more readily than any other Cabinet member. He ranked beneath the Secretary of State in the Cabinet, but Hull complained that he often acted as though 'clothed with authority . . . to shape the course of foreign policy.'

(Hull: *Memoirs*, vol. 1, p. 207)

"Over the years White brought into the Treasury, and into other branches of Government, a number of economic specialists with whom he worked very closely. White and his colleagues were in a position, therefore, to exercise on American foreign policy influence which the Diaries reveal to have been profound and unprecedented. They used their power in various ways to design and promote the so-called Morgenthau Plan for the post-war treatment of Germany. Their power was not limited to the authority officially delegated to them; rather it was inherent in their access to, and influence upon, Secretary Morgenthau and other officials, and in the opportunities they had to present or withhold information on which the policies of their superiors might be based. What makes this a unique chapter in American history is that Dr. White and several of his colleagues, the actual architects of vital national policies during those crucial years, were subsequently identified in Congressional hearings as participants in a network of Communist espionage in the very shadow of the Washington Monument. Two of them, Frank Coe and

Solomon Adler, have been for some years working for the Chinese Communists in Asia. From the Morgenthau Diaries we can glean many details of extensive political espionage operations by this group, especially in the area of policy subversion" (p. 3).

These operations, Dr. Kubek continues,

"were first intimated by Elizabeth Bentley and Whittaker Chambers in testimony before the House Committee on Un-American Activities in the summer of 1948.

"In the hearings before the Senate Internal Security Sub-committee on the operations of a Communist group within the Institute of Pacific Relations, White's name came up repeatedly. . . . Subsequently, when the Subcommittee dealt with interlocking subversion in Government departments, its hearing revealed additional data on White's activities and his connection with members of a conspiratorial Communist group operating within the Government. Dr. White was the centre of all this activity. His name was used for references by members of the espionage ring when they made application for Federal employment. He arranged their transfer from bureau to bureau, from department to department. He assigned them to international missions. He vouched for their loyalty and protected them when exposure threatened.

"When the former Communist courier Elizabeth Bentley appeared before the Subcommittee in 1952, she painted a startling picture of the fundamental design of Communist penetration. One of the two espionage groups that she 'handled in Washington' was headed by Nathan Gregory Silvermaster, an official of the Treasury Department. Concerning the avenues for placing people in strategic positions, she said: 'Two of our best ones were Harry Dexter White and Lauchlin Currie. They had an immense amount of influence and knew people, and their word would be accepted when they recommended someone.' Currie, a Canadian-born Harvard economist, fled the United States after testifying one time before the House Committee on Un-American Activities. He has lived for years in Colombia, but once had enjoyed access to the inner circle of the Roosevelt administration. He came to Washington in 1934, first to the Treasury and then to the Federal Reserve Board. In 1939 Currie was appointed as one of the six administrative assistants to the President, with special duties in economics. With Currie in the White House and White in the Treasury, the stage was set for the development of what Secretary Hull has called the 'catastrophic' programme for the post-war

disposition of Germany which came to be known as the Morgenthau Plan.
(Hull, *Memoirs*, vol. 1, pp. 207–208). (*Morgenthau Diary*, p. 4)

"Stated in its simplest terms, the objective of the Morgenthau
Plan was to de-industrialize Germany and diminish its people to
a pastoral existence once the war was won. If this could be
accomplished, the militaristic Germans would never rise again to
threaten the peace of the world. This was the justification for all
the planning, but another motive lurked behind the obvious one.
The hidden motive was unmasked in a syndicated column in
the New York *Herald Tribune* in September 1946, more than a
year after the collapse of the Germans. The real goal of the proposed condemnation of 'all of Germany to a permanent diet of
potatoes' was the Communization of the defeated nation. 'The
best way for the German people to be driven into the arms of
the Soviet Union', it was pointed out, 'was for the United States to
stand forth as the champion of indiscriminate and harsh misery
in Germany' (Issue of 5th September 1946). And so it then seemed,
for in a recent speech Foreign Minister Molotov had declared the
hope of the Soviet Union to 'transform' Germany into a 'democratic and peace-loving State which, besides its agriculture, will
have its own industry and foreign trade' (10th July 1946). Did
Russia really plan on becoming the saviour of the prostrate
Germans from the vengeful fate which the United States had
concocted for them? If this was indeed a hidden motive in the
Morgenthau Plan, what can be said of the principal planner?
Was this the motive of Harry Dexter White? Was White acting
as a Communist but without specific instructions? Was he acting
as a Soviet agent when he drafted the plan? There is no confession
in the Morgenthau Diaries in which White admits that he was
either ideologically a Communist or actively a Soviet agent. But
it is possible, given an understanding of Soviet aims in Europe,
to reconstruct from the Diaries how White and certain of his
associates in the Treasury worked assiduously to further those
aims. From the Diaries, therefore, it is possible to add significant
evidence to the testimonies of J. Edgar Hoover and Attorney
General Herbert Brownell that Harry Dexter White was ideologically a Communist and actively a Soviet agent from the day
he entered the service of the United States Government.
    "Before the entrance of the United States into World War II,
Secretary Morgenthau's principal efforts were directed at arming
the Allies against Japan and Germany. Perhaps no individual was

more committed to assisting the Allies or more ardent in furthering national defence than Morgenthau. At times Secretary Hull was fearful that Morgenthau's crusading fervour might provoke the Axis nations too far. The Diaries show sharp disagreements between the State and Treasury Departments in administering export controls and foreign funds on deposit in the United States. Morgenthau early initiated a struggle to wrest from the State Department its traditional authority over exports and imports of war material in the hope of bringing the office of Arms and Munitions Control under his department. The Secretary of the Treasury had a strong personal taste for diplomatic bargaining and was frequently engaged in discussions with ambassadors or in correspondence with foreign statesmen—activities which, of course, were properly the function of the Secretary of State. Hull warmly resented what he regarded as unwarranted interference in the field of foreign affairs" (ibid., p. 5).

The Treasury went to extraordinary lengths to acquire secret documents not related to its jurisdiction from other Departments, and the Diaries also reveal

"sharp differences between Morgenthau and the Secretary of War, H. L. Stimson, regarding the selection of personnel for postwar planning. Late in 1943 Morgenthau asked the President to name Lauchlin Currie as a representative to the European Advisory Commission meeting in London. The Commission was charged with drafting surrender terms, defining zones of occupation, and formulating plans for Allied administration of Germany. Morgenthau told the President that Currie 'would work well with the Treasury' and that 'we could surround him with three or four men 'to advise him' " (p. 6).

Silvermaster, who was later found to have organized a Communist group within the United States Government for the purpose of obtaining copies of confidential documents and other information for the Russians, was offered an important post in the Treasury Department in 1945.

"In the realm of foreign policy, Silvermaster was also active. He sent Morgenthau a memorandum on 19th June 1945, advising that the immediate problem was the 'establishing of solid Soviet-American friendship'. The man to become the next Secretary of State, he said, should be 'a liberal' and 'someone not anti-Soviet'. President Truman had been 'arduously preparing himself' for the forthcoming meeting at Potsdam with Stalin and Churchill . . .

and it would be extremely desirable if the Chief Executive could 'take a trip through the big industrial plants, mines and devastated areas of the Soviet Union'. This visit would enable the President to acquire the 'actual facts of the Soviet economy and a realistic perspective of Soviet-American trade'. Moreover a trip through the Soviet Union and Siberia would enable the President to return 'from the Big Three meeting with more intimate personal knowledge and direct personal relationship with the key people having a better knowledge than any other American and any Briton'.

"Anyone who studies the Morgenthau Diaries can hardly fail to be deeply impressed by the tremendous power which accumulated in the grasping hands of Dr. Harry Dexter White, who in 1953 was identified by J. Edgar Hoover as a Soviet espionage agent. Following the Munich crisis in the spring of 1938, Secretary Morgenthau invited White to become a regular member of the 9.30 group, made up of his principal advisers. A week after Pearl Harbour the Secretary, in a departmental order, announced that 'on and after this date, Mr. Harry D. White, Assistant to the Secretary, will assume full responsibility for all matters with which the Treasury Department has to deal having a bearing on foreign relations. . . .' The wording of this order is of the greatest significance. White's full responsibility included not only all foreign matters in which the Treasury was specifically engaged, but also any matter 'having a bearing' thereon. To a Communist agent, the opportunities this position offered were incalculable" (p. 8).

Finally, in December 1944 Morgenthau brought pressure to bear on the President to have White nominated Assistant Secretary to the Treasury.

"In order to comprehend the deplorable conditions in Germany following World War II, the influence of the Treasury in the formulation of America's postwar policy must be considered and understood. Most of the documents in the present volume concern the development of the Morgenthau Plan for the postwar control of Germany. The Diaries are full of data illustrating the influence of Harry Dexter White and his colleagues in the formulation of this detailed blueprint for the permanent elimination of Germany as a world power. The benefits which might, and did accrue to the Soviet Union as a result of such Treasury planning, were incalculable. In 1952 Elizabeth Bentley gave an extraordinarily revealing glimpse of how White's hand played a controlling part in the draft of Secretary Morgenthau's programme for the destruction of Germany. When members of the Senate Internal Security Subcommittee asked Miss Bentley whether she knew of a similar Morgenthau Plan for the Far East, she gave the Subcommittee the following testimony:

Miss Bentley: No, the only Morgenthau Plan I knew anything about was the German one.

Senator Eastland: Did you know who drew that plan?

Miss Bentley: (It was) Due to Mr. White's influence, to push the devastation of Germany because that was what the Russians wanted.

Senator Eastland: What you say is that it was a Communist plot to destroy Germany and weaken her to where she could not help us?

Miss Bentley: That is correct. She could no longer be a barrier that would protect the Western World.

Senator Eastland: And that Mr. Morgenthau, who was Secretary of the Treasury of the United States, was used by the Communist agents to promote that plot?

Miss Bentley: I am afraid so; yes.

Senator Smith: He was unsuspectingly used.

Senator Ferguson: So you have conscious and unconscious agents?

Miss Bentley: Of course. . . .

(*Morgenthau Diary*, pp. 9, 10)

"When J. Edgar Hoover testified before the Subcommittee on 17th November 1953, he affirmed this testimony. 'All information furnished by Miss Bentley which was susceptible to check', he said, 'has proven to be correct. She has been subjected to the most searching of cross-examinations; her testimony has been evaluated by juries and reviewed by the courts and has been found to be accurate'. Mr. Hoover continued: 'Miss Bentley's account of White's activities was later corroborated by Whittaker Chambers; and the documents in White's own handwriting, concerning which there can be no dispute, lend credibility to the information previously reported on White' " (ibid., p. 11).

Other officials such as Joseph J. O'Connell and Robert McConnell were engaged to draw up a programme for the control of Germany after the war, which envisaged locking up the Ruhr Valley and the removal of all its heavy industry, and some kind of "lump sum payment in the form of German material resources, German human resources and German territory. . . ." Here, then, is the basis of the so-called Morgenthau Plan which proposed to reduce Germany to

an agricultural state. As the Secretary put it, "The policy I want to
pursue, and have the Treasury pursue is, I want to let German
economy seek its own level and stew in its own juice." White liked
the simile. . . .

"The plan which Roosevelt and Churchill approved at the
Quebec Conference in September 1944 incorporated many of the
basic ideas recommended by McConnell. . . .

"In the meantime the State Department, on 31st July 1944, had
completed its own prospectus for postwar Germany. Entitled
Report on Reparation, Restitution and Property Rights—Germany,
it was diametrically opposed to the Treasury plan in that it provided for 'rapid reconstruction and rehabilitation of war-torn
areas'. There was to be no 'large-scale and permanent impairment
of all German industry'; instead it called for 'eventual integration
of Germany into the world economy' (pp. 12, 13).

"White obtained a copy of the State Department prospectus
immediately after the Bretton Woods Conference of July 1944,
probably from Frank Coe (note 41 in the text states that it might
also have been obtained from Harold Glasser). It was to prove
perhaps the most important move in his secret career as a Soviet
agent. He showed it at once to Morgenthau, who expressed the
gravest concern" (pp. 13, 14).

"Accompanied by White, the Secretary made a hurried trip
to England in August 1944, to see whether he could reverse some
of the planning then underway in the European Advisory Commission. Upon his arrival in London, Morgenthau immediately
got in touch with his personal representative on the staff of
General Eisenhower, Lt.-Col. Bernard Bernstein, an official to the
legal division of the Treasury. . . . Elated by the report that the
General was perfectly willing to 'let them stew in their own
juice', Morgenthau now had a powerful supporter whom he could
use effectively when challenging those individuals in the State or
War Departments who advocated a soft peace. On 12th August
Secretary Morgenthau called a meeting of various American
officials in London who were officially concerned with the problem of postwar Germany. In simple terms he declared . . . that the
only way to prevent a third conflagration was to make it impossible
for Germany ever to wage war again" (p. 14).

"After listening to both Morgenthau and White describe their
plan, Philip Mosely, a State Department adviser, commented that
their ideas were 'fantastic, childish and imbecilic'. Such criticism,

however, made no dent in their determination. Regardless of how others might react to their views, they made no modification. 'I thought your ideas were already crystallized by then', White said later to Morgenthau, 'and you were just trying to get their ideas and telling them your ideas'. The nature of Morgenthau's arguments made it difficult to apply a logical analysis. 'When . . . Mr. Morgenthau asserted that Germany should be converted into a purely agricultural country,' recalls Penrose in his *Economic Planning for Peace* (p. 248), 'I remarked that aside from other aspects of the question such a change was impossible because of the ratio of population to cultivable land. His rejoinder was that the surplus population should be dumped into North Africa. Such a discussion was not worth pursuing.' After his return from England, Morgenthau was visibly disturbed. The President, he thought, would have to intercede. 'He will have to get awfully busy', Morgenthau told his staff. 'There isn't anything in regard to Germany which is being carried out. I am going to tell Hull so because his boys are the worst. . . . It is going to be a nice WPA job.' Dan W. Bell agreed. He was sure, he said, that the State Department wanted to 'string out a pretty strong Germany' between the United States and Soviet Russia.

"Morgenthau now called upon Secretary Hull to tell of his experiences in London. He explained that he had asked General Eisenhower to give his view as to how the Germans should be treated after the surrender—and that the Supreme Commander had emphatically declared that Germany should 'stew in its own juice' for several months following the Allied entry" (pp. 15, 16).

"A few days later at a luncheon with Stimson, Morgenthau was horrified to learn that the Secretary of War was thinking of maintaining the social status quo in the Saar Basin under some kind of international control. . . . 'Don't you think the thing to do', he suggested, 'is to take a leaf from Hitler's book and completely remove these children from their parents and make them wards of the state, and have ex-US Army officers, English Army officers, and Russian Army officers run these schools, and have these children learn the true spirit of democracy?' When Stimson replied that he had not really given it much thought, Morgenthau announced that he was going to take the initiative in asking State, War and Treasury to work together on a plan for postwar Germany. He neglected to say that Treasury officials had been working on such a plan for more than a year.

"Early in 1944 the 'German Country Unit' was set up in

London under Supreme Headquarters, Allied Expeditionary Force (SHAEF), to draft exact plans for the military occupation of Germany . . . three drafts of a *Handbook for Military Government in Germany* were prepared . . . and a copy was probably handed to Morgenthau by his personal agent in Europe, Colonel Bernstein. The *Handbook* offered a glimpse of a very different kind of occupation than Treasury officials were hoping for. Its tone was moderate and lenient throughout" (pp. 16, 17).

However "according to an authority on the subject, 'the influence of the Morgenthau group was sufficient to hold the necessary authorization up'. (Harold Zink: *American Military Government in Germany*, p. 20) . . . Morgenthau asked White to prepare a memorandum for the President pointing out the weaknesses of the proposed programme for occupation. . . . Impressed by the memorandum, the President killed the *Handbook* and sent a stinging memorandum to Secretary Stimson, a copy of which was sent to Hull . . . concluding with the words 'The German people as a whole must have it driven home to them that the whole nation has been engaged in a lawless conspiracy against the decencies of modern civilization'. Thus both Hull and Stimson were put on notice by the President that State and War Departments must develop harsher attitudes towards Germany or be bypassed in the formulation of that policy (pp. 17, 18).

"It is indeed remarkable how the Treasury intervened and eventually got the War Department to alter its basic policy on postwar Germany. 'If we hadn't gone to England,' Morgenthau told his staff, '. . . they would have gone ahead and carried out what was in that *Handbook*" (p. 19).

"According to Lt.-Col. John Boettiger, the President's son-in-law, Bernstein was recognized throughout the European theatre as representing Morgenthau's views, and was considered an 'extremist'. He was later to be identified by the Subcommittee as a strong supporter of pro-Communist causes. He vigorously defended the Soviet Union, for example, in its methods of carrying out the Potsdam Agreement. 'Only the Russians', the *Daily Worker* of 21st February 1946 reported him as saying, 'have shown that they mean to exterminate Fascism and Nazism.'

"The influence of the Secretary of the Treasury in the making of American policy is dramatically illustrated in the unusual position held by Colonel Bernstein. Where other officials of the planning agency of the US Group Control Council in London had few direct contacts with Washington, Bernstein maintained the most intimate contacts with Morgenthau, White and other Treasury officials. He could communicate all developments in planning directly to them, and could at any time demand transportation to and from Washington. He was very active in propaganda . . . and in influencing the revision of documents in connection with the new German programme. Most of the personnel in Bernstein's office came directly from the Treasury" (p. 20).

"Another of White's protégés who played a role of some significance was Irving Kaplan, the Treasury representative on the Foreign Funds Control Section of the US Group Control Council. One of White's closest associates, he had tremendous responsibilities for American occupation policy in Germany. . . . When Kaplan went to the Treasury in June 1945, it was Frank Coe who appointed him. Coe was identified by Miss Bentley as a Soviet espionage agent" (pp. 21, 22).

"In the realm of finance, of course, the Secretary of the Treasury would naturally be involved in the postwar treatment of Germany. But Morgenthau delved deeply into matters altogether unrelated to economics (p. 22). . . . In the last few months of 1944 White kept his entire staff busy in the preparation of American policy for postwar Germany. On 28th August one of his subordinates, H. J. Bitterman, submitted a memorandum on the partitioning of Germany which included a map of the proposed division. In Bitterman's memorandum the full recognition of Soviet Russia's claim to German Territory was taken for granted.

"Recommendations by other departments on postwar treatment of Germany were constantly challenged by Treasury officials as being too soft. The State Department, for example, prepared such a draft on 1st September 1944, entitled 'American policy for Treatment of Germany after Surrender', which urged the government to decide . . . 'what kind of economic structure it proposes to leave to Germany'. If a far-reaching programme of industrial destruction or dismantlement was agreed upon, it would 'bring about extensive and important changes in European economy as a whole'. Since Germany was deficient in foodstuffs, it was doubtful that 'a plan of making Germany predominantly agricultural' could be put into effect without the liquidation or emigration of many millions of Germans. Furthermore, since Germany was an important producer of coal and bauxite for Europe, a 'wrecking programme' might have repercussions in considerable European opposition on account of its effect on the continental economy.

Moreover, if a programme of reparations was to be adopted, the destruction of German industry would make it impractical if not impossible.

"Morgenthau and White disagreed with this analysis. They were anxious to have their own programme adopted by the President before State or War could effectively interfere (p. 23).

"On 1st September the Treasury team completed a draft entitled 'Suggested Post-Surrender Programme for Germany', and rushed it to Morgenthau. . . . A few passages reveal the kind of programme that White and his associates were designing. . . . It meant the 'total destruction' of the entire German armament industry. The Ruhr should not only be 'stripped of all presently existing industries' but so 'weakened and controlled' that it could not in the foreseeable future become an effective industrial area. All its plants should either be 'completely dismantled' or 'completely destroyed', and its mines should be 'wrecked'.

"The next day White presented this draft at a meeting of State, War and Treasury officials called by Harry Hopkins in his office at the White House. Subsequently, White's draft was incorporated in the so-called Morgenthau Plan as revealed at the Quebec Conference. Essentially the plan was built on vengeance rather than on any principle of sound economics. It was quite blind in its failure to consider the fundamental fact that the victorious Allies, by striking at Germany, would be striking at the economic heart of all Europe. The economy of Europe, which had depended for generations on certain raw materials from Germany, would now be frightfully crippled. Moreover, the implementation of the Treasury plan could have no other result than to leave the Soviet Union in an unchallenged position to dominate Central Europe.

"Closely associated with White in preparing the Treasury draft was Dr. Harold Glasser, an economist in the department since 1936 (p. 24) . . . the Diaries frequently mention Glasser as contributing to the formulation of postwar schemes for the control of Germany. According to the testimony of Elizabeth Bentley, Glasser was actually a member of a Communist cell (p. 25).

"Regarding the punishment of Nazi leaders, White now suggested that a list of 'war criminals' be prepared and presented to American officers on the spot, who could properly identify the guilty and shoot them on sight. John Pehle, the Treasury lawyer, remarked that this was a fine idea, but added: 'If anything is done, it has to be done right away, or nothing will be done' " (p. 26).

Throughout the discussions Morgenthau and White incessantly came back to the plan of totally destroying the industrial resources of the Saar and Ruhr valleys. Morgenthau categorically stated that he would make the Ruhr "a ghost area" (p. 29), and that its fifteen million inhabitants could be fed out of American Army soup kitchens (p. 27).

"Such was the character of Secretary Morgenthau's views on the treatment of postwar Germany. Never in American history had there been proposed a more vindictive programme for a defeated nation. With the Treasury exerting unprecedented influence in determining American policy toward Germany, such fallacies of logic, evasion of issues and deliberate disregard of essential economic relationships were manifested in the postwar plan as finally adopted. As it resulted, no paper of any importance dealing with the occupation of Germany could be released until approved by the Treasury. The State and War Departments became virtually subservient to the Treasury in this area of their responsibility. At an interdepartmental meeting on 2nd September 1944, Harry Dexter White gave what James Riddleberger, the German expert of the Department of State, called 'a rather lengthy interpretation of his plan which, in its general tenor, was more extreme than the Treasury memorandum itself' (p. 29).

"The difference of views within the Cabinet came to a head when Harry Hopkins, the President's representative, met with Morgenthau, Stimson and Hull in the latter's office the next day. . . . While Hull favoured the elimination of Germany as a dominant economic power in Europe, he nevertheless suggested the establishment of a subsistence standard of living. Morgenthau, on the other hand, insisted that the German population be placed on a starvation diet. Stimson agreed with Hull's recommendations except that he preferred a high standard of living. 'The way to meet the Germans', he said, was through 'principles of Christianity and kindness'. Stimson's remarks aroused the wrath of Morgenthau and Hopkins, both of whom insisted upon the total elimination of Germany as a European economic factor and a less than subsistence diet for its people. Hopkins even argued against 'any steel mills at all' in postwar Germany. Stimson's persistent opposition to the Morgenthau Plan is one of the cardinal revelations of the Diaries. Dead set against the Treasury programme for 'locking up' the Ruhr, he predicted that 'thirty million people will starve if the Ruhr is closed down' (p. 30).

"On 6th September Morgenthau, Hull and Stimson met with

the President. Morgenthau continued to press for an unrelenting
policy toward Germany. . . . The President agreed that the Ruhr
should be dismantled in order that its products might be used to
'furnish raw material for the British steel industry' . . . but
Stimson came away from the meeting with a feeling that he had
made some impact on the President. Morgenthau . . . promptly
requested another meeting on 9th September.

"On 8th September Morgenthau explained to Hull 'how we got
the War Department' to change its Proclamation No. 1, a directive
to General Eisenhower. Actually the change in the proclamation
was at the suggestion of White. The first paragraph of Proclamation No. 1, as drafted by Eisenhower's staff, to be issued by General
Eisenhower upon entering Germany, read as follows:

The Allied forces serving under my command have now entered
Germany. We come as conquerors; but not as oppressors. In the
areas of Germany occupied by the forces under my command as in
other countries liberated from the horrors of Nazi tyranny, we
shall overthrow the Nazi rule, dissolve the Nazi party, and abolish
the cruel, oppressive and discriminatory laws and institutions
which the party has created. Party leaders, the Gestapo, and
others suspected of crimes and atrocities will be tried and, if
guilty, punished.

"The paragraph as drafted by the Treasury runs as follows:

The Allied forces serving under my command have now entered
Germany. We come as militant victors to ensure that Germany shall
never again (where the words were originally "drench the world
in blood" they are crossed out and written above them are the
words "plunge the world into war"). The German people must
never again become the carriers of death, horror and wanton
destruction to civilization. . . . As conquerors our aim is not
oppression but the obliteration of every vestige of Nazism and
militarism from Germany. The cruel and barbaric laws and
institutions of Nazism will be abolished. Party leaders, the Gestapo,
and those guilty of crimes and atrocities will be punished. (The
next sentence, which has been deleted, runs) Hitler and the other
arch criminals of this war will be put to death (p. 32).

"That same day White, who had the Treasury plan almost
ready in draft, advised Morgenthau on how to proceed", and told
him that Taylor, Glasser and DuBois, who were all shown to have
pro-Communist records, were working with him on the plan,
which by now they were calling the Black Book. "Morgenthau
then invited White, DuBois and Taylor to dinner . . . the Black
Book was discussed, and suggestions were offered as to how it

could be used effectively at the Quebec Conference. On 9th September Morgenthau met again with his staff before going to the White House. To make certain that he was fully briefed, Morgenthau reviewed the Black Book in detail. . . . At the President's office later that day, Morgenthau and Stimson presented their opposite views. Stimson objected vigorously to the Treasury recommendation for the wrecking of the Ruhr. 'I am unalterably opposed to such a programme', he declared (p. 33).

"When the President left Washington that same evening of 9th September for the historic meeting with Prime Minister Churchill at Quebec, he took with him a copy of the Black Book. Morgenthau accompanied Roosevelt to the railway station and then decided to ride north himself. When the train stopped overnight at Hyde Park, Morgenthau went to his own farm a few miles away. But he did not tarry long at Fishfill Hook. As Roosevelt's longtime friend he well knew how easily the President could be sidetracked, and this time no one was going to get the chance. (F. Smith, The Rise and Fall of the Morgenthau Plan, article in United Nations World, March 1947, p. 37.)

"Three days later Roosevelt wired Morgenthau : 'Please be in Quebec by Thursday, 14th September noon.' At once Morgenthau decided that White also should go. As they packed for the trip they did not neglect to include a copy of the Black Book for presentation to Lord Cherwell, one of Churchill's closest advisers.

"The plan for postwar Germany as presented at the Quebec Conference was precisely that which was outlined in the Black Book of Harry Dexter White and his associates. This plan called for a repudiation of the Atlantic Charter signed by Roosevelt and Churchill three years before. The Atlantic Charter had pledged that the United States and Great Britain would 'endeavour . . . to further the enjoyment by all states, great or small, of materials of the world which are needed for their economic prosperity'. The Treasury plan now would deprive millions of Europeans of such basic economic rights. It was Morgenthau's difficult task at Quebec to justify the plan to Churchill, who thought it far too drastic. According to Morgenthau's recollection, the Prime Minister was 'violent in the most foul language'. He declared that the American proposals were like 'chaining his body to a dead German', and were 'cruel, unchristian'. As Morgenthau hammered on the idea that the destruction of the Ruhr would create new markets for Britain after the war, Churchill gradually changed his attitude (p. 34). When Anthony Eden objected strenuously to Churchill's reversal, the Prime Minister retorted: 'If it gets down to the question of whether I am for the German people or the English people, I am for the English people, and you can be for whomever you want.' Then he added this warning: 'And I don't want you to tell the War Cabinet about Morgenthau's proposal until I get home.'

"What prompted Churchill to change his mind and accept the Treasury plan? Is it because Harry Dexter White had intimated to Lord Cherwell, who was at Churchill's side at Quebec, that if the Prime Minister approved the American plan the British could have the large loan they were seeking? Morgenthau felt that some kind of guarantee of continuing financial aid, even beyond the end of the war, was 'uppermost' in Churchill's mind. The Diaries reveal that Morgenthau himself talked with Cherwell and asked him to 'speak to Churchill' which he did, and the next morning Churchill changed his mind. Morgenthau states that the 'Memorandum on Lend-lease was not drafted until the final day and that Churchill had agreed to the policy on Germany prior to the final drafting of this memorandum' (Book 773, p. 4). Moreover, the Diaries show that Churchill was promised a loan of $6.5 billion to tide Britain over during the period from the end of the war in Europe to the surrender of Japan. Later, in a meeting with Secretary Stimson, Morgenthau denied that he had dangled such an inducement before the Prime Minister. When Stimson asked which had come first, the Treasury plan or the proposal for a loan, Morgenthau replied that Churchill 'came across' before 'we agreed' on the loan. White, who was present, remained discreetly silent, but later he reminded Morgenthau that Churchill had given his oral approval to the Treasury plan only after receiving a pledge of continuing American financial support (p. 35). . . . 'If I may remind you,' White said to Morgenthau, 'you put special stress on *when* they signed the document, but what Churchill said to the President when he was trying to get the President to agree on the document (the loan), you remember, he said: What do you want me to do, stand up and beg like Fala? And the document was signed on the Lend-lease after, but there practically was an oral commitment *before* then. It was just to be put in writing.'

"By White's own admission, therefore, Morgenthau did offer Churchill a loan in exchange for his approval of the Treasury plan for postwar Germany. But more important are these questions: Did White advise or encourage or prompt Morgenthau on how to deal with Churchill, whom he must have known would present an obstacle? What discussions did White have with

Cherwell behind the scenes? What was the precise role of White at the Quebec Conference? At present these questions cannot be answered because the official papers of the conference have yet to be published.

"Although foreign affairs and military matters were discussed in depth at the Quebec Conference, neither Hull nor Stimson were in attendance. The Treasury Department took precedence over State and War in negotiations regarding Germany. The commitments made by Roosevelt and Churchill were of greatest importance to White and his associates, who from the very beginning advocated the total destruction of Germany. To make certain that the British would fulfil their commitments under the Treasury plan, White recommended his long-time Treasury associate Frank Coe to act as secretary of the US delegation in future Lend-lease negotiations with Britain. (Coe, identified by Elizabeth Bentley as having been a member of the Silvermaster cell, subsequently fled the United States and now resides in Communist China where he writes 'agit prop' for the Chinese Communists.) The position was a critical one, since in it Coe would have control of the formulation of policy on all matters of future British Lend-lease" (p. 36).

Morgenthau summed up his success in these words:

" 'As far as I went personally, it was the high spot of my whole career in the Government. I got more personal satisfaction out of those forty-eight hours than with anything I have ever been connected with . . . the President put it this way. He said he had been groping for something, and we came along and gave him just what he wanted. But I don't know how they are going to announce it or what they are going to do about it. . . .'

"The effects of Morgenthau's victory at Quebec were quickly felt . . . and caused an irreparable division among policymakers in Washington. The old cleavage between Hull and Stimson on the one side, and Morgenthau on the other, became hopelessly deep when the President bypassed both the State and War Departments by asking the Secretary of the Treasury to present his plan at Quebec. Hull later wrote:

" 'This whole development at Quebec, I believe, angered me as much as anything that had happened during my career as Secretary of State. If the Morgenthau Plan leaked out, as it inevitably would—and shortly did—it might well mean a bitter-end German resistance that could cause the loss of thousands of American lives.' "

(Hull: *Memoirs*, vol. II, p. 1614)

"Hull felt strongly that Morgenthau should have been kept out of the field of general policy, and so did Stimson. When Stimson heard of the President's endorsement of the Treasury plan at Quebec, he quickly drafted another critical memorandum, though it must have seemed to him a waste of time to do so. Yet this refutation of the 'pastoral plan' for Germany remains the most powerful ever presented to the President (p. 37):

" '. . . I still feel that the course proposed by the Treasury would in the long run certainly defeat what we hope to attain by a complete military victory, that is, the peace of the world, and the assurance of social, economic and political stability in the world. . . . I cannot believe that they (the Treasury proposals) will make for a lasting peace. In spirit and in emphasis they are punitive, not, in my judgement, corrective or constructive. They will tend through bitterness and suffering to breed another war, not to make another war undesired by the Germans or impossible in fact . . . the question is not whether we want Germans to suffer for their sins. Many of us would like to see them suffer the tortures they have inflicted on others. The only question is whether over the years a group of seventy million educated, efficient and imaginative people can be kept within bounds on such a low level of subsistence as the Treasury proposals contemplate. I do not believe that is humanly possible. . . . Enforced poverty . . . destroys the spirit not only of the victim but debases the victor . . . it would be a crime against civilization itself.'

"Secretary Morgenthau disagreed very strongly with Stimson's views. He instructed White to study Stimson's record, while he was Secretary of State under President Hoover, in order to 'dig up' something that would indicate why he opposed the Treasury plan. 'I know he went and visited with Mussolini', Morgenthau commented briskly, because 'somebody said to me: you ought to look up Stimson's record on reparations, and you will find how bad he was, and he hasn't changed any since then' (p. 38).

"On 20th September White drafted a memorandum which Morgenthau submitted to the President. . . . Stimson, White held, completely misunderstood the Treasury plan, which was not 'punitive' but 'highly humanitarian'.

"The public reception in the United States of the so-called Morgenthau Plan was adverse but not wholly unfavourable. It was generally felt that the German people were collectively guilty of war crimes, and many Americans therefore tended to favour a hard peace. But the programme which White and Morgenthau

were advocating . . . was the most punitive which could possibly
have been designed. But could such a policy be made to stick?
The Germans would certainly resist it, and with increasing
determination as the postwar period dragged on. Was this, in fact,
the secret intention of White and his Communist friends? Did
they hope for a revolt in the Western zone of occupation in order
to make the Russians look like liberators? By identifying American
and British statesmen with what Cordell Hull called a 'catastrophic' policy, it would be possible to keep alive the hate of the
German people against the Western democracies for years to come
. . . from this angle therefore, the Treasury plan could result in
nothing but diplomatic disaster for the United States.

"By 21st September the story of the President's acceptance of
the Morgenthau Plan had leaked to the press . . . which was
almost unanimous in violent opposition to the plan" (p. 39).

In view of the forthcoming presidential elections, Morgenthau
was particularly concerned at a series of critical articles written by
Arthur Krock in the New York Times, and was puzzled as to how
the newspaper's publisher, Arthur Sulzberger, who "wants to see
the President elected", could "run a story like that." . . . Morgenthau
tried hard to find out where Krock had obtained such detailed
information on the Quebec negotiations, which were supposed to
have been secret (p. 40).

"As a result German resistance was strengthened. The Nazi
radio was shouting day and night that the Germans would become
starving peasants if they surrendered. General Marshall complained
to Morgenthau that just as the Army placed loudspeakers on the
front urging the Germans to surrender, Krock's articles appeared
and stiffened the will of the Germans to resist . . . There is no
question that the leakage to the press was disastrous to the war
effort, for nothing could have been greater in its psychological
impact upon Germany than the news of Morgenthau's coup at
Quebec in September 1944. Until then there was a fair chance,
according to intelligence reports, that the Germans might dis-
continue resistance to American and British forces while holding
the Russians at bay in the east in order to avoid the frightful fate
of a Soviet occupation. This could have shortened the war by
months and could have averted the spawning of a malignant Communism in East Germany which has plagued Europe for the past
twenty years. According to Lt.-Col. John Boettiger, the President's
son-in-law, the Morgenthau Plan was worth 'thirty divisions to
the Germans'.

"As ardent as ever in his devotion to the President, Morgenthau was increasingly worried about the reaction of the American public to his plan in the forthcoming elections. At the same time he was fearful that if all the details were revealed, the plan 'really may be hurt'. He hoped that the President would command Stimson and Hull to stop the leaks" (p. 41).

Above all he was afraid that Krock's articles would influence the President to change the plan. He thought that Krock's inference that British approval of the plan had been purchased was "so dirty" (p. 42), and he was also very upset by a letter published in the New York Times on 9th October 1944 by Calvin Hoover, recently appointed head of the Intelligence Group on the Control Council for Germany, in which he stated:

" 'The publication of Secretary Morgenthau's plan for dealing with Germany has disturbed me deeply . . . such a Carthaginian peace would leave a legacy of hate to poison international relations for generations to come . . .' (p. 42).

"This prediction of a 'legacy of hate' seemed valid, for in Germany the controlled Nazi press was having a field day. The headlines screamed: 'Morgenthau surpasses Clemenceau' and 'Roosevelt and Churchill agree at Quebec to the Jewish Murder Plan'. Hitler's chief of propaganda, Dr. Goebbels, made good use of the Morgenthau Plan as a rallying cry to the German people to put up a last-ditch resistance. This they did, for seven months more— while American bombers flattened and burned dozens of German cities and hundreds of industrial plants which American taxpayers would one day be called upon to help rebuild in order to correct the imbalance in Europe which, by a monumental miscalculation, their victory had achieved.

"The whole question of how to treat defeated Germany was in constant dispute between the Treasury and the State and the War Departments for many months. The Diaries are full of memoranda on this controversy. Yet these policy disputes encompassed much more than the fate of Germany alone; the future of the entire continent of Europe was involved . . . the acceptance of the Treasury plan by Roosevelt and Churchill at Quebec greatly strengthened Morgenthau and his colleagues during subsequent interdepartmental negotiations. They won many concessions. After the adverse press reaction, the President kept a judicious silence. He did not publicly repudiate the Treasury plan, just as he never publicly announced it. . . . Careful to give no affront to Morgenthau in his campaign speeches, the President did not commit himself beyond promising that the German people were 'not going to be enslaved'. 'Enslaved' was a word one could take as one chose. The Quebec Agreement was in fact signed only one month before President Roosevelt's address to the Foreign Policy Association in New York assuring the world that 'we bring no charge against the German race as such. The German people are not going to be enslaved—because the United Nations do not traffic in slavery'.

(G. Stolper : *German Realities*, p. 15) (p. 43)

"How the Treasury officials were able to integrate the basic features of their plan into the military directive, originally prepared by the Joint Chiefs of Staff and known as JCS 1067, is fully disclosed in the Diaries. White saw to it that many elements of his thinking were embodied in JCS 1067 . . . which General Eisenhower received upon entering Germany and which legally controlled American activities there after the surrender. However it might be read, JCS 1067 reflected the harsh philosophy of quarantine and revenge, devised and advocated by Morgenthau, White and the Treasury staff. It is very important, therefore, to grasp the fact that the revised directive of 22nd September 1944 became an official but diluted version of the Morgenthau Plan, and remained formally in effect until supplanted by a new policy directive from the Joint Chiefs of Staff in July 1947.

"In the two full years that JCS 1067 was the cornerstone of American policy in Germany, Communist infiltration into the American Military Government was a very serious problem. The harshness of the Army directive made it possible for Communist infiltration to succeed. As Germany was punished and substantially dismantled in accord with the basic tenets of the Morganthau Plan, the American zone of occupation enabled the Communists in the military-government to influence policy in the direction of Soviet desires. . . . Under the philosophy of this directive, the Germans were regarded collectively as guilty of crimes against humanity and as a menace to the world, and as such they were to be dealt with very firmly. Punishment was to be meted out to the German people as a whole by reducing their standard of living drastically (p. 44).

"JCS 1067 constituted what may be called without exaggeration a heavy millstone around the neck of the American military government. It may well rank among the most discreditable state documents ever written. . . . Immediately after the victory of Roosevelt in the November election, White and his colleagues renewed their efforts to drive through the Treasury programme for the permanent destruction of Germany. Through various channels White had gathered information concerning the kind of policy directives other departments had in preparation. This he was able to achieve through a system of 'trading' which Morgenthau had initiated at his suggestion" (p. 45).

Morgenthau requested of his collaborators that the reunions which they held together should be kept rigorously secret, except for the Russians to whom a certain amount of information was subsequently communicated. However, the Allied military became more and more insistent on the vital necessity of reconstructing German industry so that she could supply the devastated regions of Europe. But Morgenthau was kept informed of every initiative taken by the Army in this respect through the agency of high officials who had access to the most secret information.

The majority of them, such as William Henry Taylor, Harold Glasser, Frank Coe, William Ludwig Ullmann, Abraham George Silverman, Nathan Gregory Silvermaster and Lauchlin Currie were identified as belonging to the Communist network in the United States, and passed before the House Committee on Un-American Activities in 1948 and the Senate Internal Security Subcommittee in 1953.

"On 10th January 1945, Morgenthau submitted a strong memorandum to the President emphasizing Treasury fears of a new militarism in Germany . . . and went on boldly to challenge the motives of those who were opposing pastoralization. '. . . the real motive of most of those who oppose a weak Germany . . . is simply an expression of fear of Russia and Communism. It is the 20-year-old idea of a 'bulwark against Bolshevism—which was one of the factors that brought this present war down on us.' His conclusion was ominous: 'There is nothing that I can think of that can do more this moment to engender trust or distrust between the United States and Russia than the position this Government takes on the German problem' (p. 53).

"James C. Dunn, State Department political adviser on European Affairs, declared his surprise over the implication of the Treasury which charged that those who opposed the Morgenthau Plan were anti-Russian (p. 54).

"To show Morgenthau that the Treasury plan had at least the endorsement of some Soviet officials, Herbert Gaston submitted a memorandum on 25th January 1945, describing a talk with Ladimir Pravbin of TASS. . . . Pravbin's remarks had convinced him, Gaston said, that Soviet ideas on postwar treatment of Germany checked 'very closely with yours'.

"Morgenthau was not in the entourage, but Harry Hopkins, who had worked with White on the plan just before Quebec, would be at the President's side at Yalta. . . . There is no question that Churchill came to Yalta quite determined to curb the Russians; the same cannot be said of Roosevelt. The difference is that Roosevelt had been influenced strongly by the Treasury plan for postwar Germany, as concocted by White and advanced assiduously by Morgenthau for the past six months (p. 55).

"Stalin's first demand was the 'dismemberment' of Germany. . . . Roosevelt then suggested that the Big Three foreign ministers be asked to produce a scheme 'for studying the question within twenty-four hours, and a definite plan for dismemberment within a month' (W. Churchill: *Memoirs of the Second World War*, p. 915). This was faster than Churchill liked, but Roosevelt had been hearing about and looking at such a 'definite plan' for many months. It was the Treasury plan of Harry Dexter White and Secretary Morgenthau. Stalin's second demand, just as urgent, was for reparations. . . .

"Many admirers of Franklin Roosevelt have long insisted that the war-time President promptly and properly rejected the Morgenthau Plan after flirting briefly with it before and during the Quebec Conference of September 1944 (p. 56).

"The President's performance at Yalta indicates the opposite. The spirit of the Morgenthau Plan, and many of its particulars, are reflected in the decision made in the Crimea. Admiral Leahy, who was there as the President's naval aide, thought that he had witnessed 'a frightening sowing of dragon's teeth that carried germs of an appalling war of revenge at some time in the distant future' (W. Leahy: *I Was There*, pp. 322–323). In his book *Beyond Containment*, pp. 34–46, William H. Chamberlain assesses Yalta as a tragedy of appeasement: '. . . The Yalta Agreement . . . represented in two of its features the endorsement by the United States of the principal of human slavery. One of these features was the recognition that German labour could be used as a source of reparations. . . . And the agreement that Soviet citizens who were found in the Western zones of occupation should be handed over to the Soviet authorities amounted, for the many Soviet refugees who did not wish to return, to the enactment of a fugitive slave law'. This assessment is substantially correct.

"The most important proof that the Morgenthau Plan was influential at the Yalta Conference is to be found in the reaction of Treasury officials themselves to the Yalta decisions. Five weeks after the Crimea meeting Morgenthau sat down with his staff to compare the official American attitude on Germany as formulated at Quebec and at Yalta. . . . On each point Coe found the Yalta decisions compatible with and corollary to the Quebec decisions.

"After President Roosevelt returned from Yalta, State Department officials grasped an opportunity to push through their own programme for postwar Germany. On 10th March Secretary Stettinius submitted for the President's consideration the draft of a new policy directive for the military occupation of Germany. . . . Realizing that there would be fundamental objections to their programme from the Treasury, they purposely did not consult with Treasury officials. The memorandum of 10th March was a reasonable substitute for the rigorous JCS 1067 which was so pleasing to Morgenthau and White. It was based on the central concept that Germany was important to the economic recovery of Europe. It provided for joint Allied control of defeated Germany, preservation of a large part of German industry, and a 'minimum standard of living' for the German people. The memorandum had no provision for dismemberment, and Germany was to begin 'paying her own way as soon as possible' (pp. 57, 58).

"When Morgenthau saw a copy of the State Department memorandum, he became so furious that he immediately telephoned Assistant Secretary of War McCloy to voice his complaints. . . . He then complained directly to Stettinius. 'I feel that this is a completely different philosophy . . . and I can't approve it.'

"The State Department plan, if adopted, would have spelled complete defeat for Morgenthau and White. . . . For his part, Morgenthau wasted no time in getting directly to the President. He immediately ordered his colleagues to prepare a 'paragraph by paragraph' refutation showing where the State Department memorandum differed from the accepted philosophy of JCS 1067 (p. 58).

"In an emergency meeting on 19th March, Morgenthau obtained from White, Coe and Harold Glasser their best advice on how to approach the President. . . . The next day, armed with these arguments, Morgenthau hurried to the White House. He was surprised to find there Roosevelt's daughter and her husband, Major John Boettiger, whose presence evidently disturbed the Secretary very much. The Boettigers were then living at the White House and caring for the President, whose health by this time was faltering to the point where mental lapses could be expected. . . .

Did the Soviets know what the American people did not know—that Roosevelt was close to death and liable to blackouts at any moment? (p. 59).

"The next day, 21st March, an interdepartmental meeting was held for the purpose of discussing the State Department memorandum . . . and Treasury was represented by the triumvirate of Coe, Glasser and DuBois. . . . The 'major issue', as DuBois called it, ended in a resounding triumph for the Treasury on 23rd March. That day Morgenthau reported jubilantly to his colleagues that the President had been persuaded to 'recall' the State Department memorandum of 10th March, and that he had 'wholly accepted the one which was done here last night with White, Glasser and DuBois working on it' (p. 60).

"For White and his associates the President's action spelled a victory of profound importance . . . but success would not be complete, Morgenthau added, until certain people occupying key positions had been removed from the government. His concluding comment comprises a remarkably intemperate statement of his political philosophy and includes some of the strongest language to be found in the Diaries: 'It is very encouraging that we had the President to back us up . . . they tried to get him to change, and they couldn't—the State Department crowd. Sooner or later the President just has to clean his house, I mean the vicious crowd. . . . And they are for Herbert Hoover, and Herbert Hoover got us in this mess, and they are Fascists at heart . . . it is just a vicious crowd, and sooner or later they have to be rooted out. It was that crowd that fought us with no rules. . . .' The State Department was sorely disappointed that the President had rejected their 10th March memorandum (p. 61).

"A cardinal point of dispute between the Treasury and the Department of War resided in the question of the treatment of German war criminals. As early as 9th September 1944 Stimson had instructed a team of military lawyers to study in detail the possibilities of a mass trial which would prove that Nazism had developed into a conspiracy to wage a totalitarian war of aggression. Hoping to keep the President from any hasty decision on war criminals at the forthcoming Quebec Conference, Stimson carried his views to the White House. He emphasized to the President the advantage of such a trial as against the 'shoot on sight' policy advocated by Morgenthau. One of the recommendations in the Morgenthau memorandum of 6th September was that a list should be made of German archcriminals, and upon their capture and identification they should be executed at once. Contradicting this,

Stimson wrote: 'The method of dealing with these and other criminals requires careful thought and a well-defined procedure. Such procedure must embody at least the rudimentary aspects of the Bill of Rights, namely, notification of the accused of the charge, the right to be heard, and, within reasonable limits, to call witnesses in his defence' (p. 62).

"A memorandum debunking Stimson's 'legalistic position' was prepared . . . but by this time Roosevelt was dead, Truman was in the White House, and Morgenthau did not see fit to present the argument (p. 63).

"Another subject of controversy between the Treasury on the one side and State and War on the other was the question of reparations . . . the Secretary of the Treasury boldly proposed the actual cession of German territory to the victors, and the use of forced German labour to rebuild areas devastated by Hitler's armies and to work the soil of liberated countries to produce food for their peoples. Morgenthau and White were dead set against the old concept of long-term reparations payments because such annual tribute would necessitate the rebuilding of industry on a large scale in Germany. . . . On the other hand, the State Department, supported by War, advocated establishing 'widespread controls of large sectors of the German economy' . . . in order to prevent mass starvation. . . . The President had stated his wish that the German authorities, 'to the fullest extent practicable', should be ordered to proclaim and assume administration of such controls (p. 64).

"Dr. Lubin, who was appointed on 12th March 1945 (to the US delegation to the Reparations Commission), had long been interested in Russian affairs. As early as 1930, as reported in the *Daily Worker*, he had spoken under the auspices of the Friends of the Soviet Union, an organization cited as subversive by the Attorney General. . . . Lubin had known Harry Dexter White for years. . . . With the aid of his friends in the Treasury, Lubin now prepared a memorandum for the President stating that the reparations programme as advocated by the State Department would leave Germany with enough industry to recover her war potential" (p. 65).

Which provoked heated discussions with other members of the Cabinet.

"On 10th April a 'top secret' document, over the signature of DuBois, was circulated to the Department of State, War, Navy, and the Foreign Economic Administration, containing suggested provisions to be appended to the reparations directive. Among these additions was the curious concept of human reparations— the idea that a large labour force, to be supplied by the Germans 'to meet the claims of other countries' for damages, should be recruited primarily from 'Nazi groups, the Gestapo, SS organizations, officers of the Wehrmacht, and those elements of the population who have co-operated in financing and building up the Nazi machine'. A week later DuBois and Glasser reported to Morgenthau that State and War officials were attempting to prevent any 'really effective reparations programme' and had 'objected strenuously' to the Treasury argument that reparations should 'start as soon as possible' " (p. 66).

Clayton, representing State, offered the principal resistance.

"Meanwhile, on the 21st, the powerful New York financier, Bernard Baruch, acting in his capacity as adviser to the President, met with the War Cabinet and was asked where he stood on the German problem. According to Morgenthau's report to his staff, Baruch replied that his recent trip to Europe had made him much stronger for the decentralization of Germany than when he left. The Treasury plan was much too soft, Baruch said, and its author practically a 'sissy'. He would 'cut his (Clayton's) heart out if he doesn't behave himself', the financial wizard declared, adding ominously : 'he won't be able to stay around Washington after I get through with him.' Clayton had either to get 'right' on this German thing' or 'leave town'. Baruch was adamant. 'All I have got to live for now', he said, 'is to see that Germany is de-industrialized and that it's done the right way, and I won't let anybody get in my way'. He became so emotional that tears came to his eyes. 'I have never heard a man talk so strongly as he did', exulted Morgenthau, adding that he 'got the feeling from Baruch that he realizes the importance of being friendly with Russia. . . .'

"Careful not to jeopardize postwar relations with the Soviet Union, Treasury officials frequently expressed their fears of Western encirclement of Russia. On 24th April 1945, DuBois submitted a memorandum to Morgenthau describing his sympathetic views of Soviet Russia. He thought that those individuals in the American government who wished to restore Germany were motivated by the idea that a strong Reich was necessary as a 'bulwark against Russia' . . . and that this attitude was certainly responsible for many of the current difficulties between Washington and Moscow (p. 67).

"Presidential adviser Lauchlin Currie expressed similar fears of the West 'ganging up' on Russia after the war . . . a full-dress interdepartment meeting on the German question in general, and reparations in particular, was held on 3rd May in Morgenthau's office. . . . The first skirmish was over the powers of the Allied Control Council, which had been created on paper at Yalta, and in the dismantling and removal of German plants. Clayton (State) and Lovett (War) argued that a majority vote should decide all questions before the Council; the Treasury, with White speaking, insisted that such votes be unanimous, thereby leaving each ally the power of veto to prevent the removal of German industrial equipment from its particular zone. . . . The representative of State and War, on the other hand, feared that the Russian member of the Allied Control Council would prove obstreperous (p. 68). . . . Lovett wanted to be certain that the removal of industrial equipment from any of the occupied zones would not result in its eventual replacement by American tax dollars. 'Under no circumstances', he said caustically, 'should the US agree to any policy which would result in reparations being paid for by the US'.

"An even warmer dispute developed over the question of compulsory German labour as restitution for war damage in Russia. Treasury officials were boldly advocating the creation of a large labour force with no external controls, but the others vigorously disagreed with the idea of a 'slave labour force'.

"At this point Morgenthau threw the weight of his Cabinet rank into the discussion. The whole issue of compulsory labour had already been decided upon at Yalta, he announced, and somebody in the State Department 'ought to show' Crowley (of FEA) what the Yalta Agreement provided. It was no longer a question of 'whether there should or should not be slave labour'; it had been settled in the affirmative. 'We are simply carrying out the Yalta Agreement,' he exclaimed, 'and if Mr. Crowley is going to protest . . . he is protesting against Yalta . . .' (p. 69).

"Clayton was profoundly disturbed. He failed to see, he said, that the Yalta Agreement was clear as to whether the Allied armies of occupation were required to 'recruit' labourers in their zones and deliver them 'forcibly' to the Russians. To this Harold Glasser replied blandly: 'It's implied'. DuBois then reiterated what Lubin had said about the Gallup Poll showing a large per cent of Americans in favour of having 'three or four millions of Germans rebuild Russia'. But Clayton, like Lovett, was adamant in his insistence that there must be 'an international supervisory

service of some sort' to oversee the use of compulsory labour. . . .
To this suggestion Treasury officials were unanimously opposed. . . . In the crucial meeting of 3rd May even more perhaps
than ever before, Morgenthau's men were primed, confident, and
hungry for revenge on Nazi Germany. Here we see the wolfpack
of the Treasury in full cry.

"The Diaries reveal how Supreme Court Justice Robert H.
Jackson, later the chief US prosecutor at Nuremberg war crimes
trials, voiced a strong legalistic objection when he learned of the
Treasury blueprint for compulsory labour. Jackson did not think
that any person, not even a Nazi stormtrooper, ought to be
sentenced to a slave camp without first having been adjudged by
some court to be guilty. . . . Jackson held that no sentence could
be passed without trial, but the (reparations) directive did not
provide for any trial. Nor should prejudgement of these organizations be made before a trial had determined their conspiratorial
character. 'I think', Jackson said, 'the plan to impress great
numbers of labourers into foreign service, which means herding
them into concentration camps, will largely destroy the moral
position of the United States in this war. . . . In a year or two
there will come drifting out of Russia tales of oppressive treatment of this labour, which I fear will be all too well-founded
(p. 70). . . . What the world needs is not to turn one crowd out of
concentration camps and put another crowd in, but to end the
concentration camp idea'. Treasury officials were appalled by such
reasoning.

"Important as such policy decisions were, equally important
were the people who would interpret and enforce the policy
directives. It was vital that the Treasury should have one of its
most dependable men on the team of General Lucius Clay, who
would soon begin his assignment as American High Commissioner
in Germany. On 4th April 1945 General Clay had asked Morgenthau to designate a Treasury official to take full charge of the
collapsing finances of the prostrate enemy. White immediately
nominated his old friend Bernstein (p. 71). . . . For some reason
Bernstein did not receive the appointment and five weeks later
White suggested either Dr. Abraham G. Silverman or Lauchlin
Currie for the crucial post both of whom were subsequently
identified by Elizabeth Bentley and Whittaker Chambers as
belonging to a Communist cell in Washington.

"The death of Roosevelt in April 1945 brought into the White
House an executive who would quickly prove unsympathetic to
the Treasury plan for postwar Germany. Morgenthau, however,

seems to have been blissfully oblivious to the trouble ahead. . . .
He and his staff were ready to extend Treasury influence as far
and as deep as possible (p. 72).

"Fundamental changes in the management of American foreign
policy occurred after Truman became President, but these were not
clearly discernible at the time. For one thing, Truman saw to it
that the State Department soon was reasserting its proper influence in the determination of foreign policy. As the influence
of the Treasury diminished after the death of Roosevelt, a new
orientation gradually developed which was marked by a step-by-
step retreat from the principles of the Morgenthau Plan.

"On 5th July 1945, the day before President Truman left for
Potsdam, it was announced in Washington that Henry Morgenthau had resigned after eleven years as Secretary of the Treasury.
When Robert Murphy asked the President's naval aide, Admiral
Leahy, whether this sudden resignation had any special significance,
the Admiral replied: 'It's very significant. Morgenthau wanted
to come to Potsdam and threatened to resign if he was not made
a member of our delegation. Truman promptly accepted his
resignation. While the President was still a Senator, he read in
the newspapers about the Morgenthau Plan and he didn't like it.
He also felt that the Treasury was exceeding its authority in
presuming to make foreign policy. The President told us emphatically that the Treasury proposals for the treatment of Germany
are out.'

(H. S. Truman : *Year of Decision*, p. 32)

"This did not, however, prove to be quite the case. In the long
process of drafting and revising the directive to General Eisenhower . . . the spirit and indeed sometimes the letter of the Morgenthau Plan was reflected in the many mandatory provisions of the
top secret directive JCS 1067. . . . Moreover, Colonel Bernstein
and others derisively known as 'Morgenthau boys' clung to their
posts long after their chief had resigned. . . . By the end of the
year 1945 there were no less than 140 Treasury specialists in
important positions in the military government in Germany. The
weight of their considerable influence was thrown into the scales
to shift American policy in the direction which Morgenthau
had charted. As the popular columnist of the *New York Times*,
Drew Middleton, put it, the Treasury corps served as a 'counter-
weight against those officials who, because of fear of the Soviet
Union or other reasons, wanted to rebuild Germany'.

(D. Middleton : *The Struggle for Germany*, p. 47) (p. 73)

"Treatment of Germany in the 'initial control' period was the main topic discussed at the Potsdam Conference in July 1945. Allied leaders concurred in a programme which, whatever else might be said of it, mirrored the harshness of JCS 1067 and reflected the spirit of the Morgenthau Plan, particularly the idea of pastoralization. Not only were the Big Three unanimous in their conviction that German militarism and Nazism must be eradicated; they agreed also that Germany's industrial capacity was to be reduced, and the lesson of defeat brought home to every German. The Potsdam Agreement did, however, contain a clause which authorized each of the four zone commanders— American, British, French and Russian—to take any action 'essential to prevent starvation, disease, or civil unrest' in his sector. . . .

"Hardly more than a year later the Potsdam Agreement had become a subject of intense criticism. Early in September 1946, Lord Beveridge, after a visit to the British Zone of Occupation, said in a radio speech :

" 'In the black moment of anger and confusion at Potsdam in July 1945, we abandoned the Atlantic Charter of 1941, which had named as our goals for all nations improved labour standards, economic advancement, and social security; for all States, victor or vanquished, access on equal terms to the trade and to the raw materials of the world which are needed for their economic prosperity. . . . The action of the Allies for the past 15 months in Germany made the Atlantic Charter hypocrisy' (F. A. Hermans : *Potsdam or Peace*, p. 7.) Hector McNeil, Under Secretary in the British Foreign Office, was just as critical. 'To keep the German people permanently in chains', he observed, 'means to keep ourselves permanently in rags' (ibid., pp. 11–12).

"What were the final results of the Morgenthau Plan? What actual effect did it have on Germany? 'While the policy was never fully adopted', wrote W. Friedmann, 'it had a considerable influence upon American policy in the later stages of the war and during the first phase of military government. Exponents of the Morgenthau policy occupied powerful positions in military government until radical changes of American policy under Secretary Byrnes. Remnants of this policy . . . created confusion and despair among Germans.' (W. Friedmann : *The Allied Military Government of Germany*, p. 20.) This programme, largely the work of Harry Dexter White, was unquestionably the most vindictive design for a defeated enemy ever to be recommended by the US Government" (p. 75).

There is one outstanding example in which the Morgenthau and Yalta recommendations were faithfully fulfilled. The Allies had agreed to release to the Russians all nationals who were Soviet citizens, in other words, all the anti-communist Russians who had taken refuge in the English, American and French zones in central Europe, as well as all the refugees from satellite countries such as Hungary, Rumania, Bulgaria, and others. This clause was the occasion of innumerable scenes which lasted for years. At one point Soviet or ex-Soviet nationals were pursued by NKVD agents in the heart of Paris.

The French quickly realized that Russians handed over in this way would either be deported or shot, and so they took steps to see that as few as possible met this fate. The English took longer to realize the situation, but suddenly stopped handing them over. The Americans went on for a long time, and only ceased after the most atrocious tragedies had taken place, by which time their relations with the Soviets had stretched to breaking point.

"Although President Roosevelt and Prime Minister Churchill eventually recognized the folly of what they had approved at Quebec, Morgenthau, White and the Treasury staff saw to it that the spirit and substance of their plan prevailed in official policy as it was finally mirrored in the punitive directive.

"In a very definite way JCS 1067 determined the main lines of US policy in Germany for fully two years after the surrender. Beginning in the autumn of 1945, to be sure, a new drift in American policy was evident, and it eventually led to the formal repudiation of the directive in July 1947. Until it was officially revoked, however, the lower administrative echelons had to enforce its harsh provisions. Since the instructions of JCS 1067 were virtual commands, American administrators had no choice but to interpret its provisions rigidly and apply them zealously (p. 75).

"As they got around to de-nazifying one enterprise after another, they had to dismiss thousands of efficient Germans whose records placed them in categories which JCS 1067 had marked for automatic exclusion from skilled employment. A classic case was the futile attempt of the American military government to operate the railroads with untrained German personnel under the direction of the few skilled Americans available. This unhappy experiment lasted several months. It did not make US officials any happier when it was learned that many of the discharged workers immediately found jobs in the British, French or Russian zones. The British, the French and the Russians imposed no dictums in their zones comparable to JCS 1067. Their administrators, as well as many influential European journalists, viewed the American policy as utter lunacy.

"During the first two years of Allied occupation, the Treasury programme of industrial dismantlement was vigorously pursued by American officials. Industrial production was to be 'scaled down to approximately 70 to 75 per cent of 1936 levels'. . . . It was not long, however, before American officials realized that the programme implied the impossible : an economically strong Europe with a weak Germany.

"Industrial dismantlement, as it proved, worked at cross purposes with the cherished Treasury objective of pastoralizing Germany. Producers of agricultural machinery were unable to obtain legally (p. 76) the amounts of coal and iron necessary for continuous operations, and as a result many essential implements were simply not available to farmers. . . . All males between the ages of 14 and 65, and all females between 16 and 45, had to register for legal employment as a prerequisite for a food ration card. To escape the pangs of hunger, the unemployed urban population took to scouring the countryside for food and bartering away their remaining household goods. A medieval barter economy between town and country thus came into being and it did little to encourage agricultural activity.

"As White had certainly anticipated, the economic condition of Germany was desperate between 1945 and 1948. The cities remained heaps of debris, and shelter was at a premium as a relentless stream of unskilled refugees poured into the Western zones where the food ration of 1,500 calories per day was hardly sufficient to sustain life. Uncertainty regarding the future value of the Reichmark eliminated it as effective currency, and expectation of currency reform gave rise to widespread hoarding of goods. The repercussions were immediate. As Stimson, Riddleberger and others had predicted, the economic prostration of Germany now resulted in disruption of the continental trade that was essential to the prosperity of other European nations. . . . To nurse Europe back to health, the Marshall Plan was devised in 1947. It repudiated, at long last, the philosophy of the White–Morgenthau programme. The currency reforms of June 1948 changed the situation overnight. These long overdue measures removed the worst restraints, and thereupon West Germany began its phenomenal economic revival. . . .

"The Treasury plan for Germany aimed at quarantining the entire population of the defeated nation, and reducing its people

E

to abject misery. It was the absolute negation of every principle the United States held dear, and for which it had gone twice to war in one generation. Had it been carried out in its original form, it surely would have constituted the greatest act of genocide in modern history. The totalitarianism and barbarism of the Nazis were certainly enough to convince even the most charitable of Americans that only a tightly restrictive programme would effectively eliminate Germany as a threat to peace in the future (p. 77).

"After all this has been said, an implicit question haunts the historian. It is this: if the Morgenthau Plan was indeed psychopathically anti-German, was it also consciously and purposefully pro-Russian? To date, historical scholars have failed to answer, or even to ask, this vital question in their otherwise comprehensive studies of American diplomacy during and immediately following World War II. Yet this is a question of such profound historical importance that some day it must be answered definitively. The Secretary of the Treasury never denied that his plan was anti-German in both its philosophy and its projected effects, but no one in his department ever admitted that it was also pro-Russian in the same ways. In his book *And Call It Peace*, Marshall Knappen suggested in 1947 that the Morgenthau Plan 'corresponded closely to what might be presumed to be the Russian wishes on the German question' (pp. 53–56). . . . Can it be said finally that the Morgenthau Plan was Soviet-inspired? The Morgenthau Diaries alone do not yield enough incontrovertible evidence to permit an absolute pronouncement, but some of the documents published for the first time in this volume certainly point to an answer in the affirmative (p. 78).

"That Harry Dexter White was the actual architect, as well as the master builder, of the Morgenthau Plan can no longer be seriously disputed. In document after document the Diaries reveal White's abiding influence upon both the formative thinking and the final decisions of Secretary Morgenthau. Innocent of higher economics and the mysteries of international finance, the Secretary had always leaned heavily on his team of experts for all manner of general and specific recommendations. White was the captain of that team, and on the German question he called all the plays from the start. As a result of White's advice, for example, the Bureau of Engraving and Printing was ordered, in April 1944, to deliver to the Soviet Government a duplicate set of plates for the printing of the military occupation marks which were to be the legal currency of postwar Germany. The ultimate product of this fantastic decision was to greatly stimulate inflation throughout occupied Germany; and the burden of redeeming these Soviet-made marks finally fell upon American taxpayers to a grand total of more than a quarter of a billion dollars (see *Transfer of Occupation Currency Plates*—Espionage Phase, Interim Report of the Committee on Government Operations, Government Printing Office, December 1953).

"A disturbing question remains: Who or what inspired or guided the brain and hand of White? The striking similarities in both concept and detail between the Treasury plan and Soviet designs for postwar Germany may, of course, have been merely coincidental. . . . The Diaries of course do not tell the story of machinations behind the scenes on the part of White and his colleagues (p. 79).

"If in fact White was himself an active agent of Soviet espionage, as J. Edgar Hoover of the FBI has charged, the implications are profound. There can be no denial of the fact that White had wide contacts with individuals, inside and outside the government, who had in common their admiration of Marxian philosophy. Nor can it be denied that White had direct access to much of the top-secret data of the American Government. He had persuaded Morgenthau to exchange information with other departments, and by the spring of 1945 at least seven agencies were trading their confidential papers with the Secretary of the Treasury. Many of these papers inevitably crossed White's desk.

"The concentration of Communist sympathizers in the Treasury Department, and particularly the Division of Monetary Research, is now a matter of record. White was the first director of that division; those who succeeded him in the directorship were Frank Coe and Harold Glasser. Also attached to the Division of Monetary Research were William Ludwig Ullmann, Irving Kaplan, and Victor Perlo. White, Coe, Glasser, Kaplan and Perlo were all identified in sworn testimony as participants in the Communist conspiracy. . . . In his one appearance before the House Committee in 1948, White emphatically denied participation in any conspiracy. A few days later he was found dead, the apparent victim of suicide by sleeping pills (p. 80).

"Never before in American history had an unelected bureaucracy of furtive, faceless, fourth floor officials exercised such arbitrary power or cast so ominous a shadow over the future of the nation as did Harry Dexter White and his associates in the Department of the Treasury under Henry Morgenthau Jr. What they attempted to do in their curious twisting of American ideals, this fantastic decision was to greatly stimulate inflation throughout occupied Germany; and the burden of redeeming these Soviet-made marks finally fell upon American taxpayers to a grand total of more than a quarter of a billion dollars (see *Transfer of Occupation Currency Plates*—Espionage Phase, Interim Report of the Committee on Government Operations, Government Printing Office, December 1953).

"A disturbing question remains: Who or what inspired or guided the brain and hand of White? The striking similarities in both concept and detail between the Treasury plan and Soviet designs for postwar Germany may, of course, have been merely coincidental. . . . The Diaries of course do not tell the story of machinations behind the scenes on the part of White and his colleagues (p. 79).

"If in fact White was himself an active agent of Soviet espionage, as J. Edgar Hoover of the FBI has charged, the implications are profound. There can be no denial of the fact that White had wide contacts with individuals, inside and outside the government, who had in common their admiration of Marxian philosophy. Nor can it be denied that White had direct access to much of the top-secret data of the American Government. He had persuaded Morgenthau to exchange information with other departments, and by the spring of 1945 at least seven agencies were trading their confidential papers with the Secretary of the Treasury. Many of these papers inevitably crossed White's desk.

"The concentration of Communist sympathizers in the Treasury Department, and particularly the Division of Monetary Research, is now a matter of record. White was the first director of that division; those who succeeded him in the directorship were Frank Coe and Harold Glasser. Also attached to the Division of Monetary Research were William Ludwig Ullmann, Irving Kaplan, and Victor Perlo. White, Coe, Glasser, Kaplan and Perlo were all identified in sworn testimony as participants in the Communist conspiracy. . . . In his one appearance before the House Committee in 1948, White emphatically denied participation in any conspiracy. A few days later he was found dead, the apparent victim of suicide by sleeping pills (p. 80).

"Never before in American history had an unelected bureaucracy of furtive, faceless, fourth floor officials exercised such arbitrary power or cast so ominous a shadow over the future of the nation as did Harry Dexter White and his associates in the Department of the Treasury under Henry Morgenthau Jr. What they attempted to do in their curious twisting of American ideals,

Frank Coe, William Ludwig Ullmann, Abraham George Silverman, Nathan Gregory Silvermaster, Lauchlin Currie, Salomon Adler and others, were finally unmasked as secret agents working for a Soviet spy network.

White committed suicide on 16th August 1948 rather than appear before the House Committee, but after his death a dramatic confrontation about his activities took place on American television (see Chap. VIII) between President Truman and Attorney General Brownell.

As my *Judaism and the Vatican* explains in detail, during the whole of the Second Vatican Council the Jews furiously protested against the deicide accusation and against the principle of collective responsibility which this accusation entails against the Jewish people. But the Morgenthau documents clearly demonstrate that the Jews themselves applied this principle of collective guilt to Germany and pursued a policy of implacable vengeance against the whole German people whom they held responsible for Hitler's crimes and errors.

In other words, they furiously reject the principle of collective responsibility when it impugns them, but they demand its application with equal severity when they stand to become its principal beneficiaries. They won the sympathy of the civilized world for the sufferings inflicted on them by Hitler's savagely repressive measures; but thereafter they use the argument of their six million dead in order to forbid categorically any discussion of the Jewish problem. Since Nuremberg, indeed, the very word Jew has become taboo, and it can only be mentioned in the press at the risk of being described as a pogromist oneself.

As Suslov, one of the leaders of the central committee of the Communist Party in Russia, stated recently: "If you but touch so much as a single hair of any Jew anywhere in the world, all the others raise a clamour from the four corners of the globe". Just one phrase in a speech by General de Gaulle, on the occasion of the Arab-Israeli war: "The Jews, an élite people, sure of themselves and domineering"—raised a tempest of protest which was perhaps not unconnected with his fall.

Israel claims to have suffered a genocide unparalleled in history. It is true that Hitler treated the Jews without any consideration, and we are all the more ready to recognize that fact since not even the most ferocious anti-semite in France has ever suggested that the solution to the Jewish question lies in massacre and genocide. But having said this, it is nevertheless helpful to recall certain essential truths.

First of all, as regards the number of victims, six million Jews are said to have perished in the concentration camps of Auschwitz, Sobidor, Maidanek, and Treblinka, etc., all of which were situated in Poland and exclusively reserved for Jews. Six million dead, we are told, is sufficient to explain, to excuse and to justify everything.

But this figure of six million was asserted in the general hysteria which followed the Liberation at the end of the war without the slightest shadow of proof or justification. It has been widely diffused throughout the world, but today it is more and more contested, and it can be said to be akin to the famous seventy-five thousand members of the French Communist Party who were shot dead. No serious, impartial or documented study has ever been conducted on this subject, but a former inmate of Buchenwald, who was moreover a socialist, Paul Rassinier, began very far-reaching and serious research on the subject in a series of books published under the following titles: *Le mensonge d'Ulysse, Ulysse trahi par les siens, le véritable procés Eichmann and Le drame des Juifs européens* (see my *Judaism and the Vatican*, Appendix II).

He reached the conclusion that the figure of Jewish victims in the death camps hovers around the one million two hundred thousand mark, and that this figure has been more or less tacitly accepted by certain Jewish organizations such as the World Centre for Contemporary Jewish Documentation at Tel Aviv. That's a great number, and a great deal too many, especially as most of them were of little or no importance in world Jewry, but after all, Jews were not the only people to fall victim to Hitler, far from it. Hitler was responsible for the deaths of more Christians than Jews. His pitiless regime spared no one. There is the question of the treatment of the Russian prisoners, the burnt earth policy in Russia and many other brutal acts to take into consideration. The Germans themselves were among the first to fall to the regime, and quite a number of the high-up Wehrmacht leaders, soldiers covered with glory, were executed by Hitler, often with extreme savagery: General von Schleicher, Marshals Rommel, von Witzleben and von Kluge, Admiral Canaris, and some others. Their names are scarcely ever mentioned. Only Jewish victims have the power to move the universal conscience.

And then is it not true that western Jews, and those of America especially, themselves added fuel to the flames which fell on their European brothers? It is sufficient to mention the Kaufman book, to which we will refer further on, the Morgenthau documents, and the declarations of Harry Dexter White and Bernard Baruch and others, all of whom were highly influential in the conduct of the war.

The Morgenthau documents, for example, if I may remind you, were not the product of the Goebbels propaganda office, but carry an official authenticity since they were published by the Government of the United States, which may be regarded as a prototype of modern, liberal, enlightened and democratic administrations. Morgenthau and his team insistently demanded the integral application of their plan for Germany, which clearly advocated the total and definite destruction of all German industry, beginning with the Ruhr, Germany having to content herself with becoming an exclusively pastoral and agricultural country in the future.

The most immediate and obvious result of this extravagant plan would have been the deaths of thirty million inhabitants from starvation in Western Germany alone. This is precisely what the American War Minister, Stimson, promptly remarked as soon as he heard about this mad scheme, to which Roosevelt and Churchill had given their assent at Quebec. Morgenthau and his assistants were completely indifferent to this possibility. If they were pushed to the limits, Morgenthau was prepared to concede that the excess Germans should be deported to Africa.

The Morgenthau Plan also advocated three essential measures:

1. The Allies were to draw up a complete list of German war criminals who were to be arrested and shot on sight without trial.

2. Several million Germans, chosen from Nazi Party members, officers of the Wehrmacht and all those who had directly or indirectly collaborated with the regime, were to be handed over to the Russians for unconditional use as forced labour in the reconstruction of devastated areas.

3. All refugees who had fled from Soviet Russia before and during the war, would be handed over to the Russians, who would obviously either shoot them or else deport them to concentration camps in Siberia.

Morgenthau had a long and violent controversy with the Ministers of War and the State Department, who were opposed to this plan, but as long as Roosevelt was alive, he could be sure of his support and prevailed against them in securing most of his points, as the reader can see for himself by studying the résumé of the Morgenthau documents which we have published in this chapter.

The particular interest of the Morgenthau documents lies in the eminent personality of the Minister himself and the importance of the posts he held, as well as in the fact that they are official publications of the American Government. But there are other

Jewish personalities and documents which confirm and strengthen them.

As the personal friend of Roosevelt, and as the political adviser to successive Presidents of the American Republic, Baruch held a position in the Government of the United States which even surpassed that of Morgenthau in importance and influence. However, again according to the above-quoted documents, Baruch considered that the Morgenthau Plan was much too soft. All that he had got to live for, he said, was to see that Germany was de-industrialized, and turning towards the Minister of War, he added that he would not let anyone get in his way.

Both Baruch and the Morgenthau team were careful not to compromise post-war relations with the Soviet Union, and they frequently expressed their fear at seeing Russia becoming encircled by the West.

We have spent a long time on the Morgenthau documents, but they are not the only ones of their kind, and there are any number of other Jewish documents which confirm them.

From among the latter we have selected two which are more or less akin to the Morgenthau Plan : Theodore N. Kaufman's *Germany Must Perish*, which was published in 1941 in the United States by the Argyle Press, and Michael Bar-Zohar's *Les Vengeurs*, which was published by Fayard of Paris in 1968.

Kaufman's book sets out a plan which was to be applied to Germany after her defeat in order to prevent any possibility of a new war of aggression arising in the future. Kaufman advocates the total destruction of the German population by a very simple means : the massive sterilization of all men and women of German nationality between the age of puberty and 60 years.

When I first heard about this book it seemed to me such an extravagant story that I doubted its authenticity, but I finally got hold of a copy from the United States, and it is an unquestionably authentic work from which Rassinier quoted faithfully. Here are several passages from the book in question :

"Today's war is not a war against Adolf Hitler, nor is it a war against the Nazis . . . it is a struggle between the German nation and humanity (p. 1). Hitler is no more to be blamed for this German war than was the Kaiser for the last one. Nor Bismarck before the Kaiser. These men did not originate or wage Germany's wars against the world. They were merely the mirrors reflecting centuries-old inbred lust of the German nation for conquest and mass murder.

"This war is being waged by the German people. It is they who are responsible. It is they who must be made to pay for the war. Otherwise, there will always be a German war against the world (p. 2).

"This time Germany has forced a total war upon the world. As a result, she must be prepared to pay a total penalty. And there is one, and only one, such total penalty: Germany must perish forever. In fact—not in fancy (p. 3).

"There remains then but one mode of ridding the world forever of Germanism—and that is to stem the source from which issue those war-lusted souls, by preventing the people of Germany from ever again reproducing their kind. This modern method, known to science as Eugenic Sterilization, is at once practical, humane and thorough (p. 93).

"The population of Germany, excluding conquered and annexed territories, is about seventy million, almost equally divided between male and female. To achieve the purpose of German extinction (p. 94), it would only be necessary to sterilize some forty-eight million, a figure which excludes, because of their limited power to procreate, males over 60 years of age, and females over 45.

"Concerning the males subject to sterilization, the army groups, as organized units, would be the easiest and quickest to deal with. Taking twenty thousand surgeons as an arbitrary number, and on the assumption that each will perform a minimum of 25 operations daily, it would take no more than one month, at the maximum, to complete their sterilization. . . . The balance of the male civilian population of Germany could be treated within three months. Inasmuch as sterilization of women needs somewhat more time, it may be computed that the entire female population of Germany could be sterilized within a period of three years or less. Complete sterilization of both sexes, and not only one, is to be considered necessary in view of the present German doctrine that so much as one drop of true German blood constitutes a German (pp. 94, 95).

"The consequent gradual disappearance of the Germans from Europe will leave no more negative effect upon that continent than did the gradual disappearance of the Indians upon this" (p. 96).

This book is some years old, and its author is relatively unknown. Why then have we chosen to reproduce it here?

We have selected some of its passages for inclusion here because of the baneful influence the book had upon the conduct of the war. Goebbels, who had a diabolical genius for propaganda, got hold of a copy, just as he got hold of a copy of the Morgenthau Plan and the proclamation of Casablanca, in which the Allies announced to the whole world that they would demand the unconditional and global surrender of Germany, that is to say, a capitulation which would fling open the gates of Europe before Russia.

Here again I quote from the Morgenthau documents as published by the American Government:

"Hitler's chief of propaganda, Dr. Goebbels, made good use of the Morgenthau Plan as a rallying cry to the German people to put up a last-ditch resistance. This they did for seven months more— while American bombers flattened and burned dozens of German cities and hundreds of industrial plants which American tax-payers would one day be called upon to help rebuild in order to correct the imbalance in Europe which, by a monumental mis-calculation, their victory had achieved."

(Morgenthau Diary, p. 43)

It is very important to notice that Kaufman's book was published in the United States in 1941, at a time when the Jews had not yet been assembled in the death camps. It is permissible to suppose that Hitler was inspired by it when he took the decision to do away with the Jews who were in his control and who served as hostages to him in some way or other. Thus he used against them the very measures of annihilation which Kaufman and then Morgenthau and Baruch advocated against the German people.

It is almost certain that at the beginning Hitler did not intend to proceed to massacre the Jews; he wanted them out of Germany and Europe, and with this intention he began to herd them into camps with a view to transporting them when circumstances would permit.

But the war took a bad turn for Germany. Thereupon, the American Jews, Kaufman, Morgenthau and Baruch, bellowed for death and for the destruction of Germany. Thus, whether rightly or wrongly is of little importance—I am seeking to explain, not to justify—Hitler considered that he was in a legitimate state of defence. It is under these conditions that the fatal decision was taken which was to find its epilogue in Auschwitz and other camps.

Convinced by Kaufman's book, by the Morgenthau documents and by the Casablanca Conference that the defeat of Germany would herald the destruction of the country, the whole German people fought to the last with a desperate energy. As a result, the war was prolonged for one further, perfectly useless year, except that hundreds of thousands more died, and appalling destruction took place, and above all, this delay enabled communist Russia to penetrate to the heart of Europe where she is still solidly entrenched, constituting a permanent and much more serious menace to western civilization than ever did Hitler.

Long before May 1945 the Wehrmacht leaders knew that Germany had lost the war and they desperately sought to capitulate on the western front in order to protect their eastern flank from the Russians, but they were up against the demented Hitler, and the intransigent Roosevelt and Morgenthau, who were desirous at all costs of protecting the interests of their dear friends the Russians. It is in this tragic situation that the attempt against Hitler took place in July 1944.

We have just spoken of the Kaufman book, but as our readers will not be able to buy it, let us proceed at once to *Les Vengeurs* by Michael Bar-Zohar, which is readily available in all the bookshops.

Who is Michael Bar-Zohar? I have no idea. His publishers—the old and honourable house of Fayard—have this to say about him on the dust-jacket:

"Mr. Bar-Zohar was born in 1938 at Sofia in Bulgaria. He completed a brilliant course of studies at the Hebrew University of Jerusalem, and then at Paris. He is a Doctor of political science, he has an international reputation, and he has been translated and published by some of the best known firms in the United States, Germany, England, and other countries.

"Before he wrote *Les Vengeurs*, Michael Bar-Zohar travelled over the whole world, interrogating secret agents, justiciaries and judges, and examining numerous documents. . . ."

In this book, "for the first time we are presented not with the tale of the pursuit of such and such a Nazi criminal, but with a complete picture of this campaign of Jewish vengeance".

After the Allied victory and the occupation of Germany, certain Jewish groups penetrated the country, especially in the English and American zones: small Jewish military units, which had been formed within the Anglo-Saxon armies, and which consisted of interpreters, members of the Anglo-American information service, and various other ranks. This book describes their behaviour in Germany, and is obsessed with a phrase which constantly recurs throughout the work like a refrain: Jewish vengeance. We shall quote several examples of this theme from the work.

A small Jewish brigade, which had been formed into an autonomous unit within the British Army, was stationed at Brinsighella near Bologna in Italy.

"Suddenly a rumour runs through the ranks like gunpowder: we are going to be sent into Germany as part of the occupation forces. These men, these Palestinian volunteers, know that the British authorities hesitated a long time before letting them into contact with German soldiers or civilians. There was indeed reason to fear that the desire for vengeance in the Jewish soldiers was stronger than their sense of discipline. 'We are going to Germany. . . .' The men discuss the news excitedly: 'It's too good to be true.'

"We only want one month there, they said, but one month, and after that 'they' will never forget us. This time they really will have a reason for hating us. There will be just one pogrom, in round figures, a thousand houses fired, five hundred dead, a hundred women violated. . . .' And the boys were heard to say: 'I must kill a German, in cold blood, I ought to. I must have a German woman. . . . Afterwards I couldn't care less. . . . Why should we alone, we Jews, suffer Auschwitz and the Warsaw ghetto and keep all this horror in the memory of our people? The Germans, too, must be given a name to recall, that of a town which we have destroyed and blotted off the face of the earth. Our object in this war is vengeance, and not Roosevelt's four liberties or the glory of the British Empire or Stalin's ideas. Vengeance, Jewish vengeange. . . .'

"The day before departing for Germany, the call to arms took place in the Palestinian regiments. Facing the flag, a corporal read out the 'Commandments of a Hebrew soldier on German land':

Remember that the fighting Jewish brigade is a Jewish occupation force in Germany;

Remember that our appearance as a brigade, with our emblem and our flag, among the German people, is in itself a vengeance;

Carry yourself as a Jew proud of his people and of his flag;

Do not besmirch your honour with them and do not mix with them;

Do not listen to them and do not go into their houses;

May they be spurned, them and their wives and their children and their goods and everything which is theirs, spurned forever;

Remember that your mission is the salvation of the Jews, immigration to Israel and the liberation of our country;

Your duty is: devotion, fidelity and love towards the survivors of death, the survivors of the camps.

"Stock still in an impeccable position of attention, all their muscles hardened, the soldiers of the Jewish brigade listen in silence. Their impassive mien conceals feelings of hatred, mixed with an immense joy."

The Israeli writer Hanoch Bartov, who was at that time a young combatant in the brigade, later wrote:

"The blood was beating in our veins. To see our battalions drawn up under arms, and our lorries and combat vehicles ready for departure, with our flag unfurled, and to hear these words being addressed to us, all that made quite a scene. We would avenge our people, without any pleasure, without feeling any taste for the task we had to do, but we would avenge them. For all eternity we would become the implacable enemies of those who were torturing our people. And each one of us thought: 'Tomorrow, tomorrow I will be in Germany. . . .'

"The British commander decided at the last moment, in order to avoid any possibility of an incident, that the Jewish brigade would remain in Italy . . . with death in their souls, the Hebrew soldiers obeyed. The prospect of vengeance became remote. They were forbidden to go to Germany.

"Not long after the Jewish brigade arrived at Tarvisio, disorders broke out in the town: Germans were attacked, houses belonging to nazis were set on fire, women were violated. The culprits were not discovered, but the brigade command, which was formed of Jewish officers affiliated to the Hagana, became anxious. Violent disturbances of this nature were harmful to the Jewish cause. They realized that the feeling for vengeance, which ran high in all the Jewish soldiers at Tarvisio, would have to be contained, and it was with this object in mind that the leaders of the Hagana decided to entrust the right of spilling blood in the name of the whole Jewish people simply to one small group of men who were particularly reliable and known for their moral qualities".

This is the story, as told to us by one of the avengers himself:

"Our mission in this town was to be vengeance. But first of all it was essential to know whom we were intended to strike. There would have to be no doubt as to the guilt of the victims. The Hagana avengers will kill, but they will only kill deliberately. This principle was to guide all their actions.

"Their first source of information for unearthing the guilty were the Allied information services, which held dossiers of well-known war criminals and lists of SS officers and nazis living in the region. English, American and even Palestinian Jews were working in these services. 'It was they', one of the former members of the group, a man who is now a general, told me, 'who, unknown to their superiors, regularly supplied us with information'. But the dossiers and the lists were not always sufficient and they were not always available.

"By order of the Hagana, a second group of avengers was formed in the heart of the Jewish brigade. As a precaution, neither of the two commandos were aware of the existence of the other; only their leaders knew about them. Each group adopted almost identical methods. Lt.-Col. Marcel Tobias, who as a young volunteer belonged to the second group, had this to report to an Israeli journalist in 1964:

" 'The tarpaulin covered truck stopped at a pre-arranged place and on the pretext of holding a purely formal enquiry, we led out the SS officer. Behind were three soldiers of the military police who never breathed a word. When we reached a lake or a river, the SS was strangled, his body roped to a heavy stone, and he was thrown in the water. On the return journey, I left the truck two kilometres from the camp and came back on foot in order not to arouse suspicion.'

"In this way, almost every evening for months the avengers of the Jewish brigade travelled through the towns and villages of North Italy, Southern Austria and Southern Germany. They only rested when the Palestinian officers responsible for the commandos were on guard at the camp or assigned to a particular mission. Also, their punitive missions were sometimes suspended out of prudence, for rumours were beginning to circulate.

"We are not assassins. Believe me, it was not always easy.

"No, we were not afraid of danger, in fact, what we did was not dangerous. Nothing very serious could happen to us. Our deeds were not intended to serve as a warning for the future to those who might perhaps be tempted to recommence the horrors of nazism. No, these actions were secret, and they were intended to remain secret. People are not warned by the way in which we acted. Why should it not be admitted? Our action was purely and simply vengeance. Do you know the expression 'the very gentle flavour of vengeance'? That was how it felt to me, I assure you. The execution of a nazi whom I knew was either directly or indirectly responsible for snatching a baby from the arms of his mother, smashing its head against a wall, and then shooting the mother in front of the very eyes of her husband, yes, this punishment did have this very gentle and savoury taste of vengeance. I have killed. And I can tell you something else: if I had to do it again, I would. For there was a great moral justification for our actions. Since then I have never felt any remorse, not once.

"How many nazis fell at the hands of the Jewish brigade? Estimates vary, and this is understandable since the majority of the avengers only knew of the operations in which they themselves took part. According to Gil'ad, the commando was operating almost every night for six months : thus it would have accomplished about 150 executions. To this figure should be added those nazis who were discovered among the pretended sick in the hospital at Tarvisio and put to death. Another avenger who may be believed told me : 'Between two and three hundred persons'.

"But it is not essentially the number of nazis which is interesting, for whatever it may have been, it can only have been a derisory figure in comparison with the extent of their crimes and the number of their victims. It is the feelings of these men, their state of mind and the driving force behind them, which I have attempted to understand and to reveal, and I was curious to know what they thought about it all today, twenty years later.

"I have interrogated several of these avengers at length. The first conclusion which I reached is that these men, without exception, felt, at that period, that they were invested with a historic, national mission. They felt that they were representing a whole people. They are all convinced today that they acted in accordance with their duty and their obligations. Their thirst for slaking their vengeance does not appear to have affected their honesty, their moral integrity or their equilibrium. Known or unknown, almost all of them hold important civil or military posts in Israel today. They are normal men."

Most of the German victims were former nazis, SS officers, and others, which explains and in part justifies these Jewish reprisal actions, but that was not always the case, far from it, since as Bar-Zohar tells us, when for example the members of a Jewish group saw a solitary German riding his bicycle while they were out in a car, they would quickly open the door of the car when they got to him, knock him off and drive over him.

Elsewhere Bar-Zohar tells us of the Nakam group, which was formed under the auspices of the Hagana in Germany :

"The staff of the Nakam group submitted three plans for study, A, B and C.

"The principal project, said Béni, was project B. It was question of striking a massive blow against SS officers and other nazis who were assembled in the camps. We were afraid, not without reason, that they would soon be liberated, to return home unpunished. Once we had accomplished this undertaking, we would turn to plan C, which was to pursue and punish those notorious nazis whom we could track down.

"—And plan A, I asked him.

"Béni seemed a little uneasy, but eventually he told me:

"The staff of the Nakam group drew up a plan which was only communicated to a few. A great deal of time and money was spent on getting this plan into shape. This much we knew, that if it had succeeded, any other action would have been useless. Today, with the passage of time, it is permissible to describe this plan as diabolical. It involved the killing of millions of Germans; millions, I am telling you, in one go, without distinction between age or sex. The principal difficulty was that we only wanted to strike against Germans. However, the territory of the former Reich was covered with Allied soldiers and the nationals of every nation in Europe who had either been liberated from labour camps, or else had escaped from concentration camps. And then it was true that some of us had not got sufficient determination to carry out such a terrible act, even against the Germans. . . .

"As a result, we concentrated principally on plan B. After several months of research, we selected our site for action, a camp near Nuremberg—a town which had been one of the most important centres of nazism. There, thirty-six thousand SS officers had been gathered, and it was towards this camp that a little reconnaissance group made its way early in 1946 in order to carry out the first act of vengeance.

"We had decided, said Jacob, to poison the thirty-six thousand SS officers, and I was in charge of carrying out the plan.

"It did not take our agents long to find out that the camp was supplied with bread which was made by a big industrial bakery in Nuremberg which lay on the outskirts of the town near a railway line. Several thousand loaves of black and white bread were delivered to the camp every day.

"First of all we had to find out which loaves were for consumption by the prisoners, and which were destined for the Allied, American, British and Polish soldiers whose duty it was to guard the prisoners. One of our men was signed on at the bakery . . . with that knowledge, we advanced to the second stage of the plan. We took some samples of the bread and sent it to our experts.

"In their laboratories, the chemists experimented with several poisons. It was essential that it should not act too quickly, for that would have aroused their suspicion when they saw their fellow SS struck down by the bread they had just eaten.

"The group had accomplices among American soldiers of Jewish confession who were guarding the camp. By April 1946 the preparations had been completed.

"We wanted to poison fourteen thousand loaves, which would have meant six hours' work for at least five men, and two other men were also needed to keep the mixture constantly stirred in the vessel, for the arsenic had a tendency to separate from the other ingredients.

"We decided to carry out the deed one Saturday night, for two reasons : on Sunday, the bakery was shut, and the delay between the preparation of the bread and its transportation to the camp was prolonged for twenty-four hours. We chose the night of the 13th to 14th April 1946, but that night there was an extremely violent storm, the German guards and the American police remained on the alert all night, and the avengers were forced to flee in the middle of the night, although they succeeded in disguising their tracks.

"Thus operation poison loaf was a failure, but not quite, however, for the avengers had had time to make up more than two thousand loaves, and on Monday, 15th April 1946 these were taken to the camp with the ordinary loaves and distributed to the prisoners at the rate of one between five or six men. During the day, several thousand SS were violently sick, and according to the rumours which were circulated in some newspapers, twelve thousand Germans suffered as a result of eating the arsenic bread, and several thousand had died.

"These figures are exaggerated. According to the avengers, four thousand three hundred prisoners suffered from the poisoning, and about one thousand were urgently transported into the American hospitals. In the days following the incident, between seven and eight hundred prisoners died, and others, who were struck with paralysis, died in the course of the year.

"The avengers claim a total of about a thousand deaths. The American police were not long in uncovering the web. The bread led them to the factory, where they discovered the vessel containing the mixture, and all the equipment. But when it came to identifying the guilty party, their researches ended in an impasse. Terrified that the news might leak out to other prisoner of war camps, and to the civilian German population, the American commander did all he could to stifle the matter. Military censorship went so far as forbidding the German press to publish information about the poisoning."

The members of the Nakam team who had taken part in this operation succeeded in fleeing abroad, and they found refuge in France.

"They didn't stay long in France, Italy or Czechoslovakia. Once the commotion which the affair had aroused had settled down, they went back again to Germany, to continue the vengeance.

"Throughout the year 1946, however, difficulties continued to arise. The Hagana leaders and other Jewish organizations became less and less enthusiastic about the plans of the avengers.

"We felt we were being abandoned, Moshe, the leader of the Nakam group in Europe, told me. We had carried out acts of vengeance in Belgium, Holland and France. The people we met there understood our feelings better than certain Jews, better even than our Palestinian brothers. We had heart-rending discussions with people whom we imagined ought to have been of assistance to us, not excluding the Hagana.

"Certain particularly spectacular projects were opposed by the Hagana.

"Towards the end of 1945, a very far-reaching plan had been laid for executing the twenty-one accused at the Nuremberg Trial, either by poisoning them, or by letting off a bomb in the court room, or by slaughtering them while the court was in session by means of an armed commando.

"All these plans were abandoned, said Jacob, but I can tell you one thing, they were not utopian, and our preparations were very far advanced. However, we did nothing because we did not want to injure innocent people.

"Instead of proceeding with the execution of the twenty-one accused at the Nuremberg Trial, the Nakam group came back to its original plan A—the extermination, by some means or other, of several million Germans. The Hagana was aware of the risks involved in such an operation, and knew that this sort of thing could show up the Jewish people in a very unfavourable light. Accordingly it attempted to exert its authority over the group of avengers, but did the Nakam group nevertheless try and proceed with carrying out this plan?"

Whatever happened, it was dissolved and the members of the group were taken back to Palestine.

"However, at the same period, a plan for massive reprisals against the German people was on the point of coming to fruition. It was the work of a group of avengers whose peculiarity was that the majority of their members were non-Jews.

"An Israeli journalist, S. Nakdimon, was the first to bring this group to light. Other sources, whom I am pledged not to reveal, have completed the picture for me.

"These men intended first of all to set fire to several German towns. Later they laid plans for poisoning the populations of Berlin, Munich—the cradle of nazism—Nuremberg, Hamburg and Frankfort.

"Technically, the problem was not impossible. It was a question of introducing poison into the drinking water reservoirs. Here again the biggest difficulty was how to avoid injuring soldiers of the occupation forces and non-German refugees who were stationed in these five towns. It was decided to strike first at Nuremberg, where the nazis had insolently proclaimed their triumph.

"Men of our group, he told me, got themselves signed on as workmen or technicians in the companies controlling the distribution of the water. Once we had mastered the complete plan of the distribution system, we worked out a very complicated project which involved cutting off the water supplies, at zero hour, which fed the Allied occupied barracks and the areas in which most of the non-Germans were situated. These zones would have been spared, the rest of Nuremberg would have drawn poisoned water. In other words, no German ought to have survived, except the drunk. . . .

"It was not easy to get hold of the poison. A scientist from an important overseas country agreed to supply the avengers. The poison was hidden in the haversack of a soldier on leave who was returning to his unit. His mission was to hand over the haversack to a certain address in France. All was ready, but it was never carried out.

"Why not? On this point the accounts which I received do not agree.

"In describing various episodes of this strange and little known phenomenon of Jewish vengeance, I have made every effort to quote, with the minimum of comment, from the testimony which I have received. From the accounts, confidences and revelations which dozens of men have been good enough to confide to me there emerges a certain number of facts and ideas which express the peculiar and unique historical character of these reprisals.

"Let us take first of all the personalities involved. The striking thing is that all the avengers, whether from the Jewish brigade of the Nakam group, the Deutsche Abteilung, the Documentation Centre at Vienna or other groups—they were all good, honest men. Their behaviour and conduct reveal a profound intellectual and moral honesty. They were just as severe on themselves as they were on the nazi executioners. The desire for justice and their care not to strike the innocent stands out in all their acts of vengeance. As we have seen, plans for acts of massive reprisal against the German people were never carried out.

". . . and yet, when they did strike it was less to avenge a father or a brother than the whole Jewish people. Each of the avengers felt that he had been charged with a mission by all the survivors and by all the dead of the Jewish nation, a mission to punish. A mission to ensure that the men who had been responsible for massacring hundreds of defenceless men, women, old people and children, should not be allowed to return to their business in tranquillity after spending a few months in a prisoner of war camp or suffering a derisory prison sentence.

"They drowned, poisoned and shot hundreds of nazis, but they never robbed them, they never succumbed to an act of 'recuperation'. They all knew that vengeance, a blood act, had to be carried out in an irreproachable manner.

"Paradoxically, it was the creation of the State of Israel more than anything else which resulted in a lessening of this Jewish vengeance. If this Hebrew State had not had to be born, and in so doing demanded all their energy and sacrifices, it is certain that a much greater number of nazi criminals would have been executed. As has been seen, there was sometimes very acute opposition between the Palestinian Jewish organizations and the avengers. This is because these men found it difficult to choose between what they regarded as two most sacred duties—vengeance, or the creation of the State of Israel.

"The Hagana was very definitely opposed to acts of massive reprisal against the German people, in order not to arouse international opinion against the Jews, whereas the avengers would have preferred their movement to have been officially sanctioned, first of all by the Jewish organizations and subsequently by the State of Israel, so that their vengeance could be carried on in broad daylight without the need for camouflage, and so that the world would have known who was striking, and why."

(M. Bar-Zohar: *Les Vengeurs*, Paris, 1968, pp. 28–111)

These books, which are preoccupied with Jewish hatred and vengeance, leave us feeling profoundly uneasy. Besides, they clearly demonstrate that the Jewish people and the Jewish nation constitute an entity which embraces all the Jews in the world, whether of Israel, the Diaspora or Palestine. With regard to the Jews of the Diaspora, we are once again confronted with the eternal problem of dual nationality.

Genocide, assassination in concentration camps, forced labour, the murder of prisoners of war—are not these the facts which stand out in the Morgenthau Plan, in Kaufman's book and in the behaviour of Jewish groups in occupied Germany as described by Michael Bar-Zohar?

Now, between 1934 and 1945 Morgenthau and his team inspired and directed American policy towards Germany, Europe and Russia. Is one therefore to conclude that throughout this crucial period in the history of the world the might of America was put at the service of a policy dictated by Jewish hatred and vengeance?

It is a question which may validly and legitimately be asked.

VII

THE KOREAN WAR, THE SORGE SPY RING AND THE MACARTHUR-WILLOUGHBY REPORT

During the Second World War, the leading adviser to the German Ambassador in Tokyo was a man named Richard Sorge, an outstanding specialist in Japanese and Chinese affairs.

A member of the Nazi party, and the Far East correspondent of the *Frankfurter Zeitung*, Sorge, who spoke both Japanese and Chinese, had a very deep knowledge of Asian problems. He had studied the art, the religions, the politics, the literature, the traditions, the history and the economy of the two great eastern countries, he had extensive connections and possessed very exact and complete information, and his political forecasts were always proved right in the event.

The various diplomats and attachés of the Germany Embassy (military, naval, air and Gestapo), who had little experience of the problems and mentality of the east, found themselves in a country to which they were theoretically allied but which left them cut off from their own country by thousands of miles of sea and the breadth of an immense continent of land in a state of war. Germany had concluded an agreement with Japan, but in fact each country pursued its own policy without showing too much concern for the interests of its partner. Providentially, therefore, Sorge was an absolutely indispensable man whose knowledge, experience and advice was sought after on every occasion when decisions were required at the highest political level on matters affecting the German-Japanese alliance and the conduct of the war.

Sorge was on terms of the closest friendship with a Japanese called Ozaki Hozumi, a writer who was equally well versed in affairs, and who held an important position as adviser to Prince Konoyé. The latter had been Prime Minister several times and led the Japanese-American negotiations which preceded Pearl Harbour. Ozaki Hozumi was justly recognized in Japan as a great expert on Chinese questions, and by the extent of his connections and the accuracy of his judgement he represented a Japanese counterpart to Sorge. The

Sorge-Hozumi combination constituted an incomparable information service.

In October 1941 the Japanese Government sent a secret note to the German Embassy in which they revealed an absolutely staggering piece of news: Richard Sorge and Hozumi had just been arrested by the Japanese police for their part in heading a Soviet spy network. Sixteen other members of the network had been arrested at the same time, including Germans, Jews, Yugoslavians and Japanese. The Ambassador nevertheless was convinced that it was a case of appalling misunderstanding, such as had happened before in Japan, and made immediate efforts to get Sorge released, but the Japanese police held to their charge, and claimed that they had unveiled a vast spy scandal. If this was indeed the case, it was an exceptionally serious matter, and the Ambassador, Ott, and the chief of the Gestapo, Meisinger, were playing not merely for their posts but for their lives.

However, the allegations were perfectly true, and the whole matter was infinitely worse than even the most pessimistic prediction. Sorge was a Soviet agent, and with Hozumi's assistance he had organized and controlled a spy network which covered the whole of the Far East, from Shanghai to Tokyo. For nine years he had carried on these operations without awakening the least suspicions, and during that time he had passed an incredible amount of information to the Russians. The police had been alerted when a secondary member of the group, a Japanese, had denounced their activities. They had followed up the clue, and finding that it was a question of the utmost gravity, they had uncovered the whole network and then struck rapidly at a given moment.

A very lengthy and detailed enquiry then took place, lasting for three years. Once they had been arrested, Sorge, Hozumi and most of the other members of the group spoke freely. Sorge took a sort of pride in recounting the history and organization of his network in the utmost detail, describing its incredible success and its immense service to Soviet Russia. Such a tale is probably unique in the annals of international spy history, and the following is a brief resume of his account.

Richard Sorge was born in Bakou in 1895, of a Russian mother and a German father. His father was a mining engineer in the Caucasus, and his grandfather, Adolphus Sorge, had been Karl Marx's secretary at the time the first International was founded. Three times wounded in the German army during the First World War, he became a fanatical Marxist following the Russian Revolution, and a militant member of the communist party of Hamburg, where in 1920 he received a doctorate in political science. He had a natural gift for languages, and when he arrived in Japan he spoke English, French, Russian, Japanese and probably Chinese fluently. Physically, he was a very strong man, with sharp features and a violent and cruel character, given to debauchery and drink. However, he never betrayed himself among his German and Japanese drinking companions, who never knew that he also spoke Russian.

Meanwhile, Sorge became convinced that China and Japan were areas of vital importance for the future of Communism, and he set himself to study Asian problems.

In 1927 the Canton rising took place, and this event was to mark a turning point in the history of the Chinese revolution. The Kuo Ming Tan movement for the liberation of China, the successor to Sun Yat-Sen, led the struggle for the conquest of the country. Its army was commanded by the young general Tchang Kai-Chek, whose fortunes were beginning to rise. The left wing of the Kuo Ming Tan was formed by the young Chinese communist party, which was powerfully supported by Moscow under the direction of Borodin, who was in charge of political affairs, and Galen (General Blücher), who was responsible for the army. Tchang Kai-Chek was friendly disposed towards the communists and had just returned himself from a fairly long visit to Moscow.

At that time China was divided into three zones of influence: the North, which was in the hands of the war lords; the centre, with Hankow as its capital, which was in the hands of left-wing and mainly communist elements, and the South, whose capital was Nankin, which was controlled by the Kuo Ming Tan.

In April Marshal Tchang Tso Lin, Tchang Kai-Chek's ally, ransacked the Soviet Embassy at Pekin, to discover formal proof of Russian interference in the direction of the Chinese communist party and a plan to sabotage the nationalist movement. Alerted by this discovery, Tchang intercepted a secret message later in the month, which had been sent by Borodin, giving instructions as to how to sabotage the nationalist army. To put it briefly, Moscow was indeed prepared to help the Kuo Ming Tan army, but only for the eventual benefit of the communist party.

On 12th April the communists organized a general strike with a view to creating a revolutionary uprising in Shanghai. Tchang immediately seized the town and suppressed the communist movement in blood. Stalin sent Lominadze and Heinz Neumann to China in order to restore the situation. The latter, under the pseudonym of Neuberg, published the famous plan for armed communist insurrection, and at Canton insurrection was raised in the town on Neumann's personal order.

On 11th December the communists seized the town for a brief three days of terror, ransacking and massacre. Tchang immediately retook the town and suppressed the revolt in blood. Nearly all the communist leaders were shot, and the survivors gathered round Mao Tse-tung and made their way painfully south. Subsequently they undertook a dramatic retreat, the famous Long March, which led them to Yenan on the borders of Mongolia and the Russian-Chinese frontier. It seemed as if communism had been destroyed in China, and indeed it took a decade for the movement to gather way again.

It was in these conditions that Sorge was sent to China in order to reconstruct the Soviet network. He was given strict instructions to have no contact with the Chinese communist party and not to take part in any openly communist activity.

In January 1929 Sorge left for China. There he met Agnes Smedley, the famous American journalist who was a secret Soviet agent, and with her help he built up from Shanghai the base of a network which was to spread throughout the whole of the Far East, concentrating upon Japan at the time of the Second World War.

Sorge set up his headquarters at Shanghai, but spread his operations into all the big centres, notably Hankow, Nankin, Canton, Pekin and all Manchuria. He was always travelling, he learnt the Chinese and Japanese languages, he studied the history, politics, culture and philosophy of the Far East, and built up a remarkable knowledge of Asian affairs in general. He never employed a Russian, but used German, Chinese, Japanese, American and Yugoslav agents.

In December 1932, Sorge returned to Moscow in order to discuss with the Russian leaders the new situation resulting from the Japanese penetration into Manchuria and the attack on Shanghai. It was agreed that Sorge should transfer his activities to Japan and set up an entirely new spy ring there. The international situation was very grave, for Japan had invaded Manchuria, which came within the Soviet sphere of influence, and was reaching on to the Siberian frontier. An incident could set off another Russo-Japanese war, but Russia herself was in the throes of collectivization and in the West the new Hitler menace was arising. It was vital for the Russians to know the intentions of the Japanese and German governments. Accordingly, Sorge was given a supremely important mission: to find out the secret plans of the Japanese government and of the Japanese army.

In May 1933, Sorge left for Berlin in order to establish his cover story. By means of unknown influences he managed to get himself officially affiliated to the nazi party and was given a job as Eastern correspondent for the principal German papers such as the *Frankfurter Zeitung*, which already employed Agnes Smedley as its China correspondent. As they had only just come to power, the nazis had not yet perfected their redoubtable police system, and anyway there were certain to be communist agents working among their archives and records who would see to it that Sorge's communist past remained unknown. When he had got his papers in order, Sorge left for Japan via Canada and the United States, where he made contact with Soviet agents, and he disembarked at Yokohama on 6th September 1933. On presenting himself at the German Embassy and the German club he was accredited without any difficulty, and immediately the Komintern, at the request of the Red Army, began to reshuffle their agents throughout the world in order to place them at Sorge's disposition : the Yugoslav Voukelich, among others, was ordered to leave Paris for Tokyo, and the Japanese Miyagi came over from Los Angeles.

At first Sorge was simply a German newspaper correspondent of no particular importance, but he made friends with a Colonel Ott, who had just arrived in Japan. The latter knew nothing about the Far East, and Sorge's knowledge was an invaluable assistance to him. Soon Colonel Ott was made military attaché and raised to the rank of general, and finally he was appointed ambassador. Thereafter Sorge had access to the source of all official German news in Japan.

Gradually he became the ambassador's trusted adviser on all Eastern affairs. The ambassador freely showed him his official documents, exchanged points of view with him, and asked his advice, and following his example the heads of the other German missions did the same. Following the tripartite pact of September 1940, in the conclusion of which Sorge had played an important part, Germany entered into closer relations with Japan, and Sorge widened his sphere of information.

His lieutenant, Ozaki Hozumi, held an equally confidential post under Prince Konoyé, and was kept informed of the intentions and decisions of the Japanese government. Finally, owing to his position in the press, a third member of the ring, the Yugoslav journalist Voukelich, was in close contact with the English and American Embassies at Tokyo.

Sorge not merely sent back news reports to Moscow; he collected all the information which came in to him from his various sources, studied it, reflected upon it, came to an opinion about it, and finally set out his conclusions in a minutely prepared report which was sent to Moscow, and which was a mature distillation of his opinions and his personal judgement. His reports went to the highest Soviet authorities, probably to Stalin in person. What made him a truly exceptional agent was his remarkable knowledge of the East and his particular gift for distinguishing between what was important and what was not, between what was true and what was doubtful, and finally his perception and sure-footed judgement, which set an incalculable value on his personal conclusions. Here is some of the information Sorge transmitted to Russia, and I quote from General Willoughby, who was General MacArthur's chief of information services:

"From 1933 to 1935 Japanese activities in Manchuria, centring around the Chinese Eastern Railway in which the Soviet Union had a half interest, very naturally were of much concern to Moscow. Based on reports by Ozaki, Miyagi, and the then German Ambassador, Dr. Herbert von Dirksen, Sorge was able to report that Japan would not fight the USSR over the question of the Chinese Eastern Railway, would devote herself to the development of heavy industries in Manchuria, and would discuss a non-aggression pact with the Soviet Union. In fact, as Sorge was able to report on the basis of information secured through Miyagi and Ozaki in 1935, the Japanese government placed more stress on the China problem than on that of the Soviet Union and any possible advance to the North. The German-Japanese Anti-Comintern Pact of 1936 looked like the real thing, but Sorge was able to report from excellent German Embassy sources that although the Germans had wanted a military pact it was being limited to an anti-Comintern pact because of Japanese reluctance to have trouble with the USSR.

"Sorge made full reports on intentions and operations in North China after July 1937, as well as on the nature of Japanese mobilization. He transmitted Ozaki's estimate that Japan would fail in her plan to solve her North China problem by a fast campaign and that the war was bound to develop into a long struggle. Throughout the rest of the China War Sorge kept a steady flow of fundamental information to the USSR.

(Major General C. A. Willoughby: *Sorge, Soviet Master Spy,* p. 83, London, Wm. Kimber, 1952. Also published in the USA by E. P. Dutton as *Shanghai Conspiracy*)

"The European picture was very black in the spring of 1939. The USSR had a choice of negotiations either with the Anglo-French bloc or with the Germans. After they had learned from Sorge that the Germans had proposed to Tokyo, with the support of Ambassador General Oshima Hiroshi, an alliance directed against the USSR and Great Britain, but that the Cabinet, the navy and the Zaibats were all opposed to such an alliance and had blocked it, the Soviet government itself entered into the famous, and disastrous, nonaggression pact with Nazi Germany in August 1939. It was the signature of this pact, securing Hitler's Eastern frontier, which precipitated the Second World War by the invasion of Poland.

"At the time of the Nomonhan Incident, in the summer of 1939, when the Red Army and the Japanese Kwantung Army engaged in a full-scale, local war, the Red Army was able to learn Japanese intentions. They learned what units were being dispatched from what parts of Manchuria, as well as what rein-forcements would come from Japan. Above all, they learned that the Japanese government did not intend to exploit this incident, but intended to settle it locally, and the Russians conducted themselves accordingly.

"On 16th February 1940, Sorge sent a reliable account of Japanese output of munitions, aircraft, and motor cars, along with a report on the factories making these materials as well as iron and steel. From time to time, he brought these figures up to date. In August 1941 he reported on Japanese petroleum resources, a top secret bit of information of the most vital importance in estimating both Japanese war plans and capabilities. He reported that there was in storage in Japan sufficient petroleum for a two years' use by the navy, half a year by the army, and half a year by the nation at large. His sources were the German Embassy and Miyagi.

"The crucial year was 1941. After earlier general reports, on 20th May 1941, Sorge flashed the urgent warning that the Reichs-wehr would concentrate from 170 to 190 divisions on the Soviet border and on 20th June would attack along the whole frontier. The main direction of the drive would be towards Moscow. It will be recalled that this attack did occur on 22nd June. Naturally, thereafter, the answer to the question of Japanese attack from the East became the most vital mission of the Sorge ring. . . . Without a sound answer, the Red Army could not draw on their Far Eastern Army for use in the West, and, as the event showed, only a massing of limitless reserves made possible the stopping of the violent German thrusts. Sorge could not come by the answer immediately, partly because it had not been decided definitely by the responsible Japanese authorities. . . . By the end of August he reported that the German Embassy had lost hope of Japan's joining in the war against Russia in 1941.

"Sorge maintained a steady watch and reported on United States–Japanese negotiations during the summer and autumn of 1941. His information was full and accurate, since Ozaki was so close to Konoye, the key man in the negotiations (ibid., pp. 84, 85).

"By 15th October Sorge had transmitted his final sober conclusions that the Japanese had decided to move south and that there now was no serious danger of an attack by the Kwantung Army across the Siberian frontier" (ibid., p. 86).

This information was of inestimable value to the Russians. Thus alerted, they were able to withdraw from their eastern front and throw their Siberian divisions into the battle of Moscow. This marked a turning point in the war and probably sealed the fate of the German armies in Russia.

Not long afterwards, Sorge, Ozaki and all the members of their ring were arrested by the Japanese.

Once they had been arrested Sorge and Ozaki spoke freely and very fully, and gave the Japanese police complete details of their operations. They were not maltreated, and they were given every legal opportunity to present their defence. The judgement was extraordinarily mild, for only Sorge and Ozaki were condemned to death —they were hanged on 7th November 1944 at ten o'clock in the evening—and all the other members of the ring, who were given various sentences of imprisonment, were liberated as political prisoners by the American occupation troops in 1945. Miyagi and one other died in prison.

The fascination of the Sorge case lies not only in the light it threw upon the Far East, but also in the repercussions it entailed in the United States. When MacArthur's intelligence services discovered the reports of the case in the archives of the Japanese police, it was found that the names of a number of very important Soviet agents in the United States were mentioned in compromising circumstances, such as Agnes Smedley, Earl Browder, Gerhardt Eisler, Gunther Stein, and others.

The Sorge case had revealed Shanghai's importance as a centre of spying and communist agitation in the Far East. Thus alerted, the information services of General MacArthur made further enquiries and brought to light a number of very revealing facts and names.

"The Sorge story did not begin or end with Tokyo. It was no accident that Sorge served in Shanghai first, and that his later operations, localized in Japan, were only a facet in the general mosaic of Soviet and Komintern international strategy.

"Shanghai had been the focal point of Communist espionage and political subversion. . . . The miscellaneous records of the British and French Shanghai Municipal Police in the early thirties open up an astonishing vista on a fantastic array of Communist fronts, ancillary agencies, and the vast interlocking operations of the Third Internationale in China. It is in this particular period that the groundwork was laid for the Communist successes of today. . . . The role of Shanghai, a veritable witches cauldron of international intrigue, a focal point of Communist effort, already becomes apparent in the records of the Sorge trial and collateral testimony.

(General Willoughby, op. cit., p. 223)

"We are dealing here with a conspiratorial epoch in the history of modern China. China was the vineyard of Communism. Here were sown the dragon's teeth that ripened into the Red harvest of today, and the farm labour was done by men and women of many nationalities who had no personal stakes in China other than an inexplicable fanaticism for an alien cause, the Communist 'jehad' for the subjugation of the Western world (ibid., p. 225).

"The interlocking ramifications of these enterprises, on a state or national plan, can be traced on a global basis as well. This concept, of course, implies the existence of a sort of administrative general staff; we might as well accept the fact that it exists, and that its headquarters are in the Kremlin. When Sorge wanted assistants in Japan, they were summoned from all the corners of the world; when the Kremlin wanted to organize Chinese labour, British, American, French and Indian top-flight experts converged on China; when Smedley needed protection, the pink press sprang raucously to her defence; her false protestations were printed simultaneously in New York and Hong Kong. Perhaps the most striking instance is contained in the slippery meanderings of Gerhardt Eisler, almost caught in Shanghai and almost caught in New York; though fifteen years and 10,000 miles apart, Red mouthpieces then and later were ready to match their tainted skill against the judgment of government officers (ibid., p. 237).

"It can at once be stated that the individual propagandists and operators like Smedley and Stein, and the horde of saboteurs, agents, fellow travellers and dupes, unleashed by the Komintern, represents the major element in this Oriental disaster, and their nefarious work must be considered a contributory and even decisive factor. The intervention of American Communists in the Shanghai situation has been amply demonstrated . . . and unless we learn the art of self-defence in international terms, we will have the suicide of Western civilization on our hands" (ibid., pp. 255–256).

At this point, General MacArthur decided to publish the complete report of the Sorge case, with the agreement of the Minister of War at Washington, who had read and approved the text.

Then an incredible thing happened. The American progressives and Communists, realizing that they were directly implicated, reacted with extreme violence, and thereupon the official authorities in Washington disowned the report of Generals MacArthur and Willoughby.

"The news value of the Sorge story is self-evident; even more so its importance as a pattern of Soviet intelligence operation. In December 1948, the Secretary of the Army had taken steps to clear the story for release.

"The American press was thoroughly interested. In the normal course of events, following the initial release, the papers were waiting for further details, in particular for the release of documentary evidence, the confessions of the principal defendants, participants, and eye-witnesses.

"G–2 Tokyo was prepared to furnish this material, but the call never came. Instead, a few days later, a shocked and incredulous Headquarters, in Tokyo, became aware of what amounted to a virtual repudiation of the Sorge Spy Report by the very Washington authorities who had so eagerly negotiated for its release throughout an entire year.

"This official reversal was reflected in the staccato language of news service radios of the period :

WASHINGTON, 20TH FEB.: (INS): THE ARMY'S PUBLIC INFORMA-TION DIVISION SAID FLATLY SATURDAY THAT IT WAS WRONG AND IN ERROR IN CHARGING THAT AGNES SMEDLEY, AN AMERICAN WRITER, WAS A RUSSIAN SPY.

EYSTER SAID "THE DIVISION HAS NO PROOF TO BACK UP THE SPY CHARGES. THE REPORT WAS BASED ON INFORMATION FROM THE JAPANESE POLICE AND THE REPORT SHOULD HAVE SAID SO.

"WHILE THERE MAY BE EVIDENCE IN EXISTENCE TO SUBSTANTIATE THE ALLEGATIONS, IT IS NOT IN OUR HANDS.

"IT WAS A MISTAKE WITHIN THE DIVISION. THE STAFF FAILED TO
HANDLE THE RELEASE PROPERLY. NO NAMES SHOULD HAVE BEEN
USED AND NO CHARGES MADE."
WASHINGTON, 19TH FEB. (UP) IN NEW YORK, MISS SMEDLEY
PROMPTLY CALLED THE CHARGES "DESPICABLE LIES" AND THERE
WERE OTHERS WHO CRITICIZED THE ARMY'S METHOD OF BRINGING
OUT THIS REPORT.

"The Army Department retraction was certain to cool off the
eagerness of the press immediately.

"The direct practical effect of this inexplicable step was to
suppress for the time being documentary evidence that normally
would have reached the public. *Plain Talk* and *Counterattack*
were among the first to recognize the vicious impact of this
retraction.

"Agnes Smedley significantly got space on the air, hired a
well-known attorney, and proceeded to defend her fair name. It
was a foregone conclusion that this would be done. The implications of international conspiracy, in the Far East, were too over-
whelming. Silence would have been fatal for the cause of Soviet
penetration of the Orient, especially as the Chinese Communists
were then already at the gates of Nanking.

"The psychological counterattack was cleverly managed. It was
primarily directed at General MacArthur and its weapon was an
insolent threat of suit for libel. The magic of MacArthur's name
would automatically insure front space in the press. The fact that
the release was a Washington-directed affair was blandly over-
looked. Nor was there any point in suing me, though the direct
responsibility for the preparation of the report, i.e. the substance
of accusation, was obviously in my department.

"Agnes Smedley expressed her gratitude and appreciation to the
Army for clearing her name and reputation of the outrageous and
false charge. She hoped that the statement by Colonel Eyster
'marks the end of a policy of smear first—investigate later.' She
called upon General MacArthur 'to waive his immunity and she
would sue him for libel.' In Detroit, John Rogge, attorney for
Smedley, asked rhetorically: '. . . First we want to know if
MacArthur will accept responsibility for reports coming from
his office, and if he will, I suggest he get a New York lawyer
because we are going to sue. After we get an answer from Mac-
Arthur, then we will decide whether to sue Willoughby. Mac-
Arthur is the one Miss Smedley wants to sue. . . .'

"In order to relieve Rogge of this theatrical dilemma, I immediately issued a public broadcast, in which I accepted suit with the deliberate intent, of course, of forcing the evidence into the open.

'. . . *The Sorge Spy Report, collating and evaluating certain judicial and other official records found in Japan at the start of the Occupation, was made under my sole direction and, as Chief of Military Intelligence Section, Tokyo, I am responsible for its preparation and direct transmission to the Military Intelligence Division in Washington.*

'*I accept fully any responsibility involved and waive any immunities I may possess, to legal or any other action that may be taken or desired. I would in fact welcome, not only as an Intelligence Officer but even more fundamentally as an American citizen, an opportunity thus to emphasize the lurking dangers which threaten American Civilization in subversive systems, hiding behind and protected by our free institutions. . . .*'

"The statement above, broadcast on the evening of 21st February, is not an ordinary action. It represents the public acceptance of a challenge, despite the fact that the official agencies in Washington appeared to side with an international espionage agent against a general officer of thirty-five years of continuous honourable military service.

"This length of military service obviously involves a certain amount of disciplined resignation. Officers do not lightly enter into a controversy with the War Department. . . .

"Traditional loyalty to superior authority, silent obedience, etc., were all involved in this scandalous incident, when the Sorge Espionage Case, an authenticated intelligence report, was released with considerable fanfare but retracted within seventy-two hours with quasi-apologies that ranged from an admission of editorial mistakes to the much more damaging innuendo that there was neither proof on hand nor any evidence to substantiate the allegations.

"As a matter of public safety, as well as government integrity, it is important to know why Smedley received the inferential protection of the Department and of the Secretary of the Army. It should be noted that from the hour of my broadcast, Smedley and her mouthpiece lapsed into complete and cautious silence. Incidentally, John Rogge, Smedley's lawyer, appears to handle a number of 'Red' cases. It is suggestive of his intellectual attitude that he demanded an end to the New York Grand Jury investigations into Soviet espionage activities. . . ."

F

(Major General Willoughby : *Sorge, Soviet Master Spy*, pp. 197–200)

... "After Washington had suppressed the proffered documentation, G–2 Tokyo found the going rough; the pack was in full cry; 'pink' riff-raff of every category, several second-rate columnists on the outer fringe of journalistic respectability, and a few opportunist politicians joined forces (ibid., p. 201). ... Communist publications, magazines and periodicals the world over rallied to the cause of Agnes Smedley while she was still alive. Her protest against the Army release of the Sorge Report was featured on 8th March 1949, by a mouthpiece for Chinese Communism, the *China Digest*, published in Hong Kong. At a distance of 10,000 miles, another Communist front, the *Far East Spotlight*, featured her story on practically the same date. This perfect timing, over vast geographical areas, is an impressive example of the first-class general staff work and split-second co-ordination of international Communism. The propaganda work of the timid and vacillating democracies cannot match this deadly precision" (ibid., p. 203).

Who then was this Agnes Smedley at the centre of all this commotion?

For twenty years she was one of the most ardent propagandists on behalf of communist China, and in this capacity she exercised a vast influence on American public opinion, for it was she who propagated the fable that the Chinese communists were moderates who simply wanted to carry out agrarian reforms. Likewise, she was responsible for the sympathetic attitude towards communism of General Stilwell, who at that time was the American government's representative to Tchang Kai-Chek, before the latter's final defeat in China, and as we have seen, she belonged to the Sorge spy ring, and introduced him to Ozaki.

Agnes Smedley was born in Missouri in 1894 of a poor family. In 1912 she married an engineer, whom she divorced shortly afterwards. She then took a course at the University of New York, where she joined a group of Hindu nationalists. In 1918 she was arrested with Rabindranath Ghose, a political agitator, but the case never came to court. In 1920 she joined another professional Hindu revolutionary named Virendranath Chattopadhyaya, and lived with him for eight years. In 1928 she broke off relations with him and went to China as the correspondent of the *Frankfurter Zeitung*, and in 1929 she took up residence at Shanghai, where French and British police records reveal that she was acting as an agent of the komintern. It was at Shanghai that she became friendly with notorious Communists, such as C. Frank Glass, Harold Isaacs, Irene Wedemeyer, and Anna Louise Strong and others.

In 1933 she published a propaganda book in support of the Chinese communists entitled *China's Red Army Marches*, which included an account of Mao Tse-tung's "Long March" across China. It was banned by the nationalist Chinese authorities and by the Europeans at Shanghai on account of its violent attack on the opponents of Communism. Smedley had written it in a Soviet welfare centre in the Caucasus, where she had been receiving treatment for her health. In 1934 she travelled to Europe, returning to Shanghai the following year.

In August 1937 she went to Yenan, the capital of the Chinese communists, and became friendly with Chou En-Lai and above all with Chu Teh, who was commander of the 8th Chinese communist army. From this moment she unreservedly supported the cause of the Chinese communist armies, whose operations she followed across the country. In 1941 she fell ill and went to Hong Kong, and then returned to America where she conducted a very active propaganda campaign in favour of the Chinese communists.

In 1949, she crossed swords in a bitter encounter with MacArthur over the publication of the Sorge Report, but she was careful not to get involved in a case which would have brought out too much about her past. In 1950, just at the moment when she was due to appear before the commission of enquiry on Un-American activities, she left hastily for London where she died suddenly in a clinic. She had nominated Chu Teh as her universal legatee, and her ashes were sent to China and buried with great ceremony in a cemetery at Pekin which shortly afterwards fell into the hands of Mao-Tse tung.

And here we now set before the reader the final conclusion on the Sorge case as stated by General MacArthur in his reply to the memoirs of President Truman (translated from the French):

"The following events were probably finally responsible for my dismissal. In January I demanded that an enquiry should be opened in order to destroy a spy network which was responsible for the treasonable leakage of my ultra-secret reports to Washington. My campaign plans, including those of the 8th Army, were being daily communicated to Washington. General Walker was constantly complaining to me that the enemy had been informed of all his movements in advance. No such leakage occurred in Korea or Japan. Then suddenly one of my reports concerning the order of battle was published in a newspaper in

Washington several hours after it had been received. I insisted that those responsible should be brought to justice, in order to prevent the recurrence of this sort of thing, but nothing was done, and shortly afterwards I was relieved of my command.

"It is only quite recently, following the revelations which came out in the Burgess-Maclean spy trial, that I began to realize exactly what had been happening. These men, who had access to top secret government documents, were indisputable links in the spy chain which stretched from Washington to Korea, via Pekin and Moscow. I am convinced that my demand for an enquiry, which followed on the heels of the Alger Hiss and Harry Dexter White scandals, caused the liveliest resentment in government circles and was considered an anti-democratic manœuvre.

"I am equally convinced that Red China's decision to launch an attack on Korea was undertaken with the assurance, provided from Moscow (through its American spy ring), that this measure would not draw down reprisals against the Chinese armies' bases and lines of communication in Manchuria. I do not want to cast a doubt upon the loyalty and patriotism of President Truman, but his obstinacy in refusing to admit the danger of red infiltration, and the way he sought to discredit as a red-herring any attempt to unmask this peril, is a staggering feature of this period."

(*US News and World Report*, issue of 17th February 1956)

To finish this chapter, we will briefly summarize the conclusions which may be drawn from these spy trials.

Firstly, the communists consider that they are in a state of permanent war with the rest of the world. This war is both revolutionary and totalitarian, and it is conducted on all fronts at once: it is military, political, scientific, industrial, commercial, artistic, and above all, philosophical and religious. At the same time, this permanent war is also a civil war. There is an interior front within all the western countries which is just as important if not more so than the exterior front, and the three main weapons of communism in this internal front are the official Communist Party, the underground networks and the support of liberals and progressives.

To take the Communist Party, this organization is a legally constituted entity free to carry out its antinational activity in broad daylight. It is in fact a fifth column in the service of a foreign government which itself is in a state of cold war with the western world.

The underground networks have four main tasks: to supply

information to the Soviet government, which is regarded as the world centre of the revolutionary movement; to set up cells within and infiltrate the western governments in order to exercise a political influence over them which is all the more efficient as it is secret; to set up cells within and infiltrate the different industries of the country in preparation for war and revolution by means of sabotage; and secretly to form groups ready to take power, which is the essential object of all the communist parties throughout the world.

With regard to the liberals and the progressives, as we have seen in the course of their trials, the communist agents are recruited from liberal and progressive intellectual circles, which possess in common, often unconsciously, an affinity of ideas and sympathies, and a sort of tacit alliance. Most of the agents to whom we have referred by name in this book were not even communists in the true sense of the word, and in this capacity they were often more useful to the Party than if they had in fact been members. They were not poor people, but intellectuals who had come from big Universities such as Cambridge in England, or Harvard and Colombia in the United States, or McGill in Canada. Many were often very gifted persons who commanded important posts, and some, such as Noel Field of the Vanderbilt family in America, or Raymond Boyer in Canada, were very rich.

As Chambers remarked, in the United States the working classes are democratic, the middle classes are republican and the upper classes and the intellectuals are communists. That is a fact which is not always sufficiently well grasped, but it is nevertheless more often true than not.

The existence of progressive circles facilitates the work of recruiting agents, and broadens its scope. It also assists the underground network of cells in their work of spying and collecting information, infiltrating and setting up cells in the government, and in the formation of new cells.

Furthermore, it is particularly efficacious in helping agents in difficulties arising from political enquiries or court cases.

When Alger Hiss was charged with spying, a number of well-known personalities took up his defence before public opinion, including Felix Frankfurter, a Justice of the Supreme Court, Dean Acheson, who was then in the State Department, and Truman, President of the Republic.

The Rosenbergs, also in America, were defended in front of public opinion by two of the most well-known scientists in the States: Einstein and Urey. Besides, a world-wide agitation in their favour was unleashed against the American government.

When General MacArthur denounced the American writer Agnes Smedley from the evidence revealed in the documents of the Sorge case, he was repudiated by his own Minister of War, who publicly defended Smedley against him, and when the General attempted to attack the progressive circles which surrounded Smedley, he was purely and simply dismissed.

Let us refer once more to the case of Carol Weiss King, the lawyer who was the recognized defendant of communists brought up on a charge before the American courts :

"Carol Weiss King and her law partner, the late Joseph R. Brodsky . . . played an exceedingly important role in the organization and direction of a wide variety of communist legal aid fronts in this country. The high level on which this lady operates is indicated by the fact that she has acted as counsel for Earl Browder, Israel Amter, Robert Minor, Sam Carr, of the Canadian espionage apparatus, Harry Bridges, Jay Peter, and the Eisler brothers, Hans and Gerhardt. She was also a contact for Hede Massing (Gumperz), when the latter was a Soviet agent in New York. . . . She got the Eislers into the country in the first place. Hans was held up in Cuba as a known Communist. An appeal was made to Mrs. Roosevelt, who appealed to the State Department. When the Consulate in Cuba remained firm, he was moved into Mexico and got in through that easy gateway."

(Maj.-Gen. C. A. Willoughby : *Sorge, Soviet Master Spy*, pp. 239–240)

Here was an instance of Mrs. Roosevelt intervening in person in favour of a communist agitator at the request of Carol Weiss King.

There was another typical case which had fairly wide publicity at the time, the *Amerasia* affair.

"Philip Jaffe, author of a pro-Communist book boosted by the *New York Times* . . . was the editor of the magazine called *Amerasia*. He had been intimate with Earl Browder, who had singled him out to influence American public opinion on the side of Red China. . . . *Amerasia* continued in existence until 1945 with a small circulation insufficient to pay the cost of printing.

"In that year it became involved in an incident which almost defies belief. There appeared in *Amerasia* a long account which was recognized in General William Donovan's Office of Strategic Services (the OSS) as an almost word for word reproduction from a government document of top secrecy. How did this get out. . . ? The head of the OSS investigating service entered the offices of

Amerasia magazine, by picking the lock, and found on the desks and in the files an alarming array of documents still bearing the top-secret mark of the State and other departments. They were from Military Intelligence, Naval Intelligence, Bureau of Censorship, British Intelligence, Office of Strategic Services and the State Department. The case was turned over to the FBI. Its agents, after working on the case for three months, swooped down on the *Amerasia* offices on 6th June 1945. They recovered 1,800 government documents stolen from the secret files of many war agencies of the government . . . all these facts were given to a grand jury which on 10th August brought in an indictment against Jaffe, Larsen and Roth. . . .

"How could the government have a clearer case than this? By this time the honeymoon between the United States and Russia was at an end. Yet here was an officer in Naval Intelligence (Roth) and a research agent in the State Department (Larsen) . . . involved at least suspiciously with two outright Communists who were running a pro-Communist magazine with their offices stuffed with stolen secret documents from the State and other departments, including Naval and Military Intelligence. . . . Among these documents were military reports giving secret information on the position and disposition of Chinese Nationalist armies—a subject of the greatest importance to the Communist military leaders in China. This was not a case of a single secret document gone astray. It was a whole officeful from many departments—a job which could have been carried on only through a long period of thefts by many hands.

"Now, the most startling feature of this case was its climax. The original indictments were quashed. Instead of charges of espionage, the charge of 'conspiracy to embezzle' was substituted against Jaffe, Larsen and Roth. Then Jaffe's attorney and the government's attorney got together and agreed on a swift court procedure. The government attorney said little. The defendants meant no harm . . . it was all a case of excessive journalistic zeal. Imagine an ordinary loyal newspaper reporter stealing 1,800 secret government documents just to check on the accuracy of his story. . . ! The judge actually heard almost nothing about the case. He fined Jaffe $2,500. Larsen got off with a $500 fine. The case against Roth was dismissed . . . the government expressed the hope that the matter might be wound up without further delay, which was done. Of course, all this fantastic procedure took place on orders from Washington."

(J. T. Flynn : *While You Slept*, pp. 108–110)

"Now, what was the truth about *Amerasia*. . . ? Actually, it was projected and organized in the Institute of Pacific Relations . . . which belonged to the Communists Field and Jaffe . . . it was hardly a magazine at all. It was a front posing as a magazine which could be used as a safe cache for secret government documents and as a clearing house for secret government information . . . as we survey the IPR record no one can doubt that it played a powerful role in our State Department, and it is not out of place to note that Alger Hiss became a member of the board of the IPR. . . . Major General C. A. Willoughby testified under oath that the IPR Council in Japan was used as a spy ring by the Russians."

(J. T. Flynn, ibid., pp. 110-112)

And that brings us to the conclusion of this study. The supreme danger is not from Communism in Moscow or Pekin; the supreme danger lies in infiltration from underground networks in Paris, London and Washington, and in the secret links which bind them to liberal and progressive circles.

In June 1951, General MacArthur made a speech to the members of the Texas Legislature, in the course of which he stated:

"I am much concerned for the security of our great nation, not so much because of any potential threat from without, but because of the insidious forces working from within which, opposed to all of our great traditions, have gravely weakened the structure and tone of our American way of life."

(quoted in J. Beaty: *The Iron Curtain over America*, p. 193)

Finally, we will bring this chapter to its close with a quotation from J. T. Flynn:

"It is difficult to believe that so few people, so little known, without political influence on the nation as a whole, could accomplish so much. The trick lies in getting into positions where information can be controlled, where policies can be formed, getting into strategic spots where the switches which govern information, opinion and policy can be controlled. Take the case of Alger Hiss in the State Department and Harry Dexter White in the Treasury Department. There was Hiss at Yalta, White at Quebec, where world-shaking decisions were made to conform to Russian plans. All of these people comprised not more than 35 or 40 men and women—most of them writers and journalists, some of them Communist Party members or agents of some Communist apparatus, many of them mere dupes. They managed to write most of the books and most of the book reviews, while taking their places in positions of the greatest strategic importance in departments of the government—State and War and Navy and OWI and other sensitive agencies. Think of the power of Lauchlin Currie in the President's own executive department as his adviser on Far Eastern affairs—Currie who was in the IPR and was identified by Elizabeth Bentley as a member of the Communist Silvermaster group in Washington. Think of Hiss, top-ranking man in the policy committee of the State Department. Think of Lattimore, adviser to Chiang Kai-shek—on Currie's recommendation—at a critical moment, adviser to the State Department, adviser to Wallace on his visit to Siberia and China. Think of Frederick Vanderbilt Field as executive secretary of the IPR, of John Carter Vincent as head of the Far Eastern Division of the State Department, and a score of others we could name. These are the men and women who were able to change the course of history and embroil us in the fantastic snarl in which we find ourselves in the Far East."

(J. T. Flynn : *While You Slept*, p. 115)

"It is easy enough to diagnose the case of those men who were outright Communists or half-convinced fellow travellers. They knew what they believed and what they were aiming at. The trouble lies in tracing the illness which possessed the minds of men who were neither Communists nor Socialists, yet who could be afflicted with some disorder that brought them down to a point where they saw our problems almost precisely as the Reds saw them, and led them to become, in some cases the deluded, and in some cases the completely blind partner of the enemy. These aberrations led to a shockingly false conception of the war and its objectives and its meanings. In turn, by the most gigantic propaganda assault in history, they set out to fool the American people about the war and its purposes.

"While we arm against Russia, we remain defenceless against the enemies within the walls. It is they, not Stalin's flyers or soldiers or atomic bombers, who will destroy us."

(J. T. Flynn, ibid., pp. 151, 152)

VIII

THE BROWNELL-TRUMAN CONTROVERSY

The Soviet spy drama, which had come to light with the revelations of Elizabeth Bentley and Whittaker Chambers, did not end with the condemnation of Alger Hiss. It was to crop up again in a most spectacular manner several years later, in connection with Harry Dexter White, but this time ex-President Truman was directly implicated.

As the reader will remember, Harry Dexter White, a Jew of either Polish or Russian origin who had been naturalized as an American, was denounced by Whittaker Chambers as being one of the leaders of a Soviet spy ring in the United States. He had held a very important post in the Treasury and in the International Monetary Fund which had played such an important part in the economic measures taken by America with regard to Europe at the end of the Second World War. White died in 1948 a few days after making his only appearance before the House Committee on Un-American Activities which was investigating the Hiss affair. Truman was President of the United States at the time.

On 6th November 1953, the Attorney General of the United States (the Minister of Justice), Herbert Brownell Jr., stated publicly in a speech at Chicago that ex-President Harry Truman had at that time nominated Harry Dexter White to a post of the utmost importance, knowing perfectly well all the time that White was a communist agent.

Naturally, this allegation created a considerable stir.

Ten days later, Harry Truman himself was shown throughout America on a gigantic programme which was simultaneously broadcast by the four big television companies, and in which he presented his version of the story.

The complete text of this broadcast was published in France by the Paris edition of the New York Herald Tribune on 18th November 1953.

On the previous day, 17th November, Brownell had appeared before the Committee of Enquiry of the United States Senate and given a detailed explanation of the White affair which he had unveiled on 6th November, and on the same day J. Edgar Hoover of the Federal Bureau of Investigation made a long statement to the same Committee on this subject.

Both Brownell and Hoover were very hard on ex-President Truman, and made formal accusations against him with supporting evidence.

These two statements were reproduced in full in the Paris edition of the *New York Herald Tribune* on 19th November 1953, and the same issue set out in rather ponderous terms the general conclusions which could be drawn from these three statements, and which likewise contained severe strictures against the former President.

Quoting from the respective editions of the *New York Herald Tribune* as indicated above, we will now set out an abridged version of the three statements; commencing with the television broadcast of former President Harry S. Truman:

"On 6th November, the new Administration, through Herbert Brownell Jr. . . . now serving as Attorney General, made a personal attack on me. . . . This attack is without parallel, I believe, in the history of our country. I have been accused in effect, of knowingly betraying the security of the United States. This charge is, of course, a falsehood, and the man who made it had every reason to know it is a falsehood. On 10th November, as a direct result of this charge, I was served with a subpoena of the House Committee on Un-American Activities, which called on me to appear before it to be questioned about my conduct of the office of the President of the United States. . . ."

Truman then explained at length why he refused to appear before the House Committee.

"Now for the charge which Mr. Brownell made in his political speech—a charge that I knowingly betrayed the security of the United States. Let me read you what Mr. Brownell said. Mr. Brownell said: 'Harry Dexter White was known to be a communist spy by the very people who appointed him to the most sensitive and important position he ever held in the government service.' There can't be any doubt that Mr. Brownell was talking about me. . . .

"His charge is false, and Mr. Brownell must have known it was false at the time he was making it.

"Mr. Brownell has made a great show of detail as to the dates on which particular FBI reports were forwarded by the Department of justice and the manner in which they were handled. As

Mr. Brownell should have learned by this time, a great many reports pass daily through the White House. It is not possible to recall eight years later the precise day or the precise document which may have been brought to my attention. . . .

"But of course I knew of the intensive investigation of Communist activity which was then going on and which involved many persons. As a matter of fact this investigation was one of the many important steps which my Administration took, beginning in 1945, to render the Communist conspiracy ineffective in this country. These steps included the successful prosecution and imprisonment of the top Communist leaders in the United States. . . .

"I have had my files examined and have consulted with some of my colleagues who worked with me on this matter during my term in office. The facts, as I have determined them in this matter, are these : in late 1945, the FBI was engaged in a secret investigation of subversive activities in this country. In this investigation, the FBI was making an intensive effort to verify and corroborate certain accusations of espionage made by confidential informants.

"A lengthy FBI report on this matter was sent to the White House in December 1945. The report contained many names of persons in and out of government service, concerning whom there were then unverified accusations. Among the many names mentioned, I now find, was that of Harry Dexter White, who had been in the Treasury Department for many years and who was at that time an Assistant Secretary of the Treasury. As best I can now determine, I first learned of the accusations against White early in February 1946, when an FBI report specifically discussing activities of Harry Dexter White was brought to my attention.

"The February report was delivered to me by Gen. Vaughan and was also brought to my personal attention by Secretary of State Byrnes.

"This report showed that serious accusations had been made against White, but it pointed out that it would be practically impossible to prove those charges with the evidence then at hand.

"Immediately after the matter was brought to my attention, I sent a copy of the report, with a covering note signed by me, to White's immediate superior, the Secretary of the Treasury, Fred Vinson. In this note, dated 6th February 1946, I said : 'I suggest that you read it, keeping it entirely confidential and then, I think, you, the Secretary of State and myself should discuss the situation and find out what we should do.' Later, I believe it was the same day, I discussed the matter with Secretary Vinson as well as with Secretary of State Byrnes.

"As I have mentioned, Mr. White was at that time an Assistant Secretary of the Treasury. It had been planned for some time that he should be transferred from that position to be the United States member on the board of executive directors of the International Monetary Fund, a new international organization then in the process of being set up. His appointment had been sent to the Senate for this new position, and it was confirmed on 6th February shortly before I saw Secretaries Byrnes and Vinson. In this situation I requested Secretary Vinson to consult with the appropriate officials of the government and come back to me with a recommendation.

"Secretary of the Treasury Vinson consulted with Attorney General Tom Clark and other government officials. When the results of these consultations were reported to me, the conclusion was reached that the appointment should be allowed to take its normal course. The final responsibility for this decision, of course, was mine. The reason for this decision was that the charges which had been made to the FBI against Mr. White also involved many other persons.

"Hundreds of FBI agents were engaged in investigating the charges against those who had been accused. It was of great importance to the nation that this investigation be continued in order to prove or disprove these charges and to determine if still other persons were implicated.

"An unusual action with respect to Mr. White's appointment might well have alerted all the persons involved to the fact that the investigation was under way and thus endanger the success of the investigation. It was originally planned that the United States would support Mr. White for election to the top managerial position in the International Monetary Fund—that of managing director—a more important post than that of a member of the board of executive directors. But following the receipt of the FBI report and the consultations with members of my Cabinet, it was decided that he would be limited to membership on the board of directors.

"With his duties thus restricted, he would be subject to the supervision of the Secretary of the Treasury, and his position would be less important and much less sensitive—if it were sensitive at all—than the position then held by him as Assistant Secretary of the Treasury.

"Tonight I want the American people to understand that the course we took protected the public interest and security and, at the same time, permitted the intensive FBI investigation then in progress to go forward. No other course could have served both of these purposes. The appointment was accordingly allowed to go through, and the investigation continued. In 1947 the results of the investigation up to that time were laid before a Federal Grand Jury in New York by the Department of Justice. Mr. White was one of the witnesses called before that grand jury. . . . In the meantime, Mr. White, in April 1947, resigned his office, referring to reasons of health."

Then the former President Truman launched into an extremely violent diatribe against Brownell, whom he accused of attacking him in bad faith in order to discredit the democratic administration in favour of the republican party.

"The whole history of our Republic", Truman continued, "does not reveal any other attack such as this by a new administration on an outgoing President. Up to now, no administration has ever accused a former President of disloyalty. . . . It is now evident that the present administration has fully embraced, for political advantage, McCarthyism. I am not referring to the Senator from Wisconsin—he's only important in that his name has taken a dictionary meaning in the world. It is the corruption of truth, the abandonment of our historical devotion to fair play. It is the abandonment of the law. It is the use of the big lie and the unfounded accusation against any American citizen in the name of Americanism or security. It is the rise to power of the demagogue who lives on untruth. It is the spread of fear and the destruction of faith in every level of our society.

"My friends, this is not a partisan matter. This horrible cancer is feasting at the vitals of America and it can destroy the great edifice of freedom. If this sordid, deliberate and unprecedented attack on the loyalty of a former President of the United States will serve to alert the people to the terrible danger that our nation and every citizen faces, then it will have been a blessing in disguise. I hope this will arouse you to fight this evil at every level of our national life."

(*New York Herald Tribune*, Paris, 18th November 1953)

Those are his very words. This horrible cancer, this terrible danger which threatens the American nation—what is it but McCarthy's anticommunism.

On 17th November 1953 the Attorney General replied to President Truman's speech with a statement which was made before the Senate Internal Security Subcommittee, from which we have extracted the most important passages as follows :

"Beginning in April 1953, this subcommittee has been holding a series of hearings for the purpose of exposing the plans of Communist agents to infiltrate the government of the United States. The work of this subcommittee has documented with great care the result of the very successful Communist espionage penetration in our government during World War II and thereafter. . . . The Executive department of the government, which is headed by the President, and of which the Department of Justice is part, has been concerned since we took office with cleaning out the government. One of the most important and vital problems is to remove all persons of doubtful loyalty and, most important, to prevent any further Communist infiltration into the government of the United States.

"On 6th November in Chicago, I made one of a number of speeches and magazine articles in which I publicly discussed the problem of Communist infiltration in government and the steps taken by the Eisenhower administration to meet that problem. In that speech I referred to the case of Harry Dexter White and the manner in which it was handled by the Truman administration on the basis of established facts and the records in the Department of Justice.

"It has been said that I implied the possibility that the former President of the United States was disloyal. I intended no such inference to be drawn. . . . I specifically said that I believed that the disregard of the evidence in the White case was 'because of the unwillingness of the non-Communists in responsible positions to face the facts and a persistent delusion that Communism in the government of the United States was only a red herring', and that 'the manner in which the established facts concerning White's disloyalty were disregarded is typical of the blindness which afflicted the former administration on this matter'.

"When this subcommittee completes its investigation, I believe that you will conclude, as I did, that there was an unwillingness on the part of Mr. Truman and others around him to face the facts and a persistent delusion that Communist espionage in high places in our government was a red herring. And I believe that you will conclude that this attitude, this delusion, may have resulted in great harm to our nation.

"The Truman administration was put on notice at least as early as December 1945, that there were two spy rings operating within our government. . . . White entered upon his duties and assumed the office of executive director for the United States in the International Monetary Fund on 1st May 1946. What was known at the White House of his espionage activities prior to that date?

"On 4th December 1945, the FBI transmitted to Brig.-General Harry H. Vaughan, military aide to the President, a report on the general aspects of Soviet espionage in the United States. . . . This was a secret and highly important report of some 71 pages. It covered the entire subject of Soviet espionage in this country both before, during and after World War II. It named many names and described numerous Soviet espionage organizations. Harry Dexter White and the espionage ring of which he was a part were among those referred to in this report . . . no reasonable person can deny that the summary, brief though it may be, constituted adequate warning to anyone who read it of the extreme danger to the country in appointing White to the International Monetary Fund or continuing him in government in any capacity, as the subcommittee knows.

"Copies of this report were sent to a number of Cabinet officers and high officials in the Truman administration, including the Attorney General. It would be difficult to understand how, under any circumstances, a document upon so delicate and dangerous a subject would not have been brought to Mr. Truman's attention.

"But in addition to the fact I have here a letter from J. Edgar Hoover to General Vaughan dated 8th November 1945. As you know, General Vaughan has testified before this subcommittee that by arrangement with Mr. Truman, when the FBI had information which it deemed important for the President to know about, it sent such information to him. Vaughan testified that he knew that any such report which came to him was delivered to the President."

Mr. Brownell then read out the contents of this letter, in which Hoover, the head of the FBI, drew Vaughan's attention to the importance of the report which accompanied it. The names of a certain number of persons who were Soviet agents, and all of whom occupied posts in the American government, were mentioned, especially Harry Dexter White, Gregory Silvermaster, George Silverman, Frank Coe, Laughlin Currie, Victor Perlow, Maurice Halperin and others; all these men were cited in the Chambers–Hiss trial.

The report stated that according to a confidential source of information, which had reached the FBI, Harry Dexter White had been active as a spy since 1942, and that the documents which he had obtained had been photographed in a secret laboratory in a cellar in Silvermaster's house. A special messenger then took the photographs to Jacob Golos and Gaik Ovakinian, two other Soviet agents who completed the link. Golos died on 27th November 1943, and thereafter the link was maintained by Dr. Abraham Weinstein and Anatole Gromov, who was first secretary in the Soviet Embassy in Washington.

Hoover also remarked that if White was nominated executive director of the International Monetary Fund he would be able to exert a great influence over all questions concerning international finance, and he added that he would not be able to keep him under effective surveillance since the offices of the International Monetary Fund were regarded as neutral international territory, and consequently FBI agents were not allowed to enter them.

Continuing his deposition, Mr. Brownell referred to the existence of a second FBI report which completed the first and which was especially concerned with White's spying activities since the end of 1945. To this day this report is still too secret for complete publication, but it mentioned White's frequent contacts with men who were known to be notorious communists by the FBI, and his close relations with Alger Hiss were also mentioned, as well as the *Amerasia* case, to which we will refer later on.

Mr. Brownell concluded his deposition with these words:

"No one could, with any validity, suggest today that there is doubt that White was in this espionage ring. Some of White's original espionage reports, written by him in his own hand-writing for delivery to agents of the Red Army intelligence, were recovered in the autumn of 1948 and are now in the possession of the Department of Justice. . . . But the record which was available to the Truman administration in December 1945 and thereafter should have been sufficient to convince anyone that White was a hazard to our government.

"The question which had to be decided at that time was not whether White could have been convicted of treason. There was ample evidence that he was not loyal to the interests of our country. That was enough. Government employment is a privilege, not a right, and we don't have to wait until a man is convicted of treason before we can remove him from a position of trust and confidence. . . .

"However it now seems in the light of Mr. Truman's television speech of last night that it is conceded that on 6th February 1946, the day on which White's appointment was confirmed by the Senate, Mr. Truman did read the most important of the reports to which I referred, and that he thereafter, even though he had a legal right to ask that the nomination be withdrawn, signed White's commission and permitted him to take office on the 1st May with full knowledge of the facts reported by the FBI.

"It is of course extraordinary to learn from Mr. Truman, in view of his earlier statements, that he signed Mr. White's commission with the thought that it might help to catch him . . . it seems to me even more extraordinary to learn that Mr. Truman was aware as early as 1946 that a Communist spy ring was operating within his own administration, when for so many years since that time he had been telling the American people exactly the opposite. Indeed, it seems to me that this explanation of White's appointment—that is, that he was appointed and allowed to remain in office for more than a year in order to help the FBI trap him as a spy—raises more questions than it answers."

(*New York Herald Tribune*, Paris, 18th November 1953)

On 18th November, J. Edgar Hoover, director of the Federal Bureau of Investigation, made the following statement before the Senate Internal Security subcommittee. Hoover began by recalling that the FBI is a fact-finding agency and is not concerned with making decisions of policy. Its role is to supply the government with the information relative to the security of the country, and thereafter it is the latter's responsibility to take the decisions which it considers to be necessary. Hoover then continued:

"On 7th November 1945, Miss Elizabeth Bentley advised special agents of the FBI in considerable detail of her own career as an espionage agent. On 8th November a letter of that date was delivered to Brig.-General H. H. Vaughan", which listed a certain number of persons who were working as Soviet agents. "Harry Dexter White was the second name mentioned in the list. The concluding paragraph of this three-page letter stated: 'Investigation of this matter is being pushed vigorously, but I thought you would be interested in having the foregoing data immediately.'

"In the meantime, our investigation of White and other members mentioned by Miss Bentley and Whittaker Chambers, as well as those individuals on whom we had adverse information from equally reliable sources, continued. A detailed summary memorandum was then prepared consisting of 71 pages, exclusive of the index, setting forth the highlights of Soviet espionage in the United States. This memorandum, dated 27th November 1945, was delivered to General Vaughan by a special messenger on 4th December 1945. Copies of this memorandum were furnished to the Attorney General and certain other interested heads of government agencies. This memorandum included information on Harry Dexter White.

"When we learned that White's name had been sent to the Senate for confirmation of his appointment as a United States delegate on the International Monetary Fund, we then consolidated the information in our files . . . in a 28-page summary dated 1st February 1946, which was delivered to General Vaughan on 4th February 1946.

"From 8th November 1945 until 24th July 1946, seven communications went to the White House bearing on espionage activities, wherein White's name was specifically mentioned. During that same period, two summaries on Soviet espionage activities went to the Treasury Department and six went to the Attorney General on the same subject matter. The handling and reporting on the White case followed the bureau's traditional practice of reporting all facts and information which had come to our attention, without evaluation or conclusions.

"The information contained in the summary delivered to General Vaughan on 4th February 1946 came from a total of 30 sources, the reliability of which had previously been established. In connection with the sources, I would like to mention one in particular, Miss Bentley. From the very outset, we established that she had been in a position to report the facts relative to Soviet espionage which she has done. We knew she was in contact with a top-ranking Soviet espionage agent, Anatoli Gromov, the First Secretary of the Soviet Embassy in Washington.

"All information furnished by Miss Bentley, which was susceptible to check, was proven to be correct. She has been subjected to the most searching of cross-examinations. Her testimony has been evaluated by juries and reviewed by the courts and has been found to be accurate. Miss Bentley's account of White's activities was later corroborated by Whittaker Chambers and the documents in White's own handwriting, concerning which there can be no dispute, lend credibility to the information previously reported on White. Subsequent to White's death, on 16th August 1948, events transpired which produced facts of an uncontradictable nature which clearly established the reliability of the information furnished in 1945 and 1946.

"In the period from 8th November 1945 to 22nd February 1946, our first concern was to safeguard the government from infiltration by subversive elements. In fact, I took a strong stand because of the premature disclosures that would result if prosecution were initiated.

"In a conversation on 21st February 1946, the Attorney General informed me that he had spoken with the then Secretary of the Treasury, the late Chief Justice Fred Vinson, and the President, about White. The Attorney General stated he felt the President should personally tell White that it would be best for him not to serve. I told the Attorney General I felt it was unwise for White to serve. The Attorney General then stated he would like to confer with Judge Vinson and me on the following day.

"I advised Judge Vinson and the Attorney General that the character of the evidence was such that it should not be publicly disclosed at that time in view of the confidential sources involved. . . . I was at the meeting to furnish facts, which I did. There was no agreement while I was present between the Attorney General and Judge Vinson, other than that they should see the President with the Secretary of State.

"On 26th February 1946, I advised the Attorney General by telephone and subsequently by memorandum, of the receipt of information from a confidential source reflecting the possibility that White might have received some notice of either the cancellation or impending cancellation of his appointment.

"Mr. Virginius Frank Coe, a close associate of White's, became the secretary of the International Monetary Fund in June 1946, which position he held until 3rd December 1952, when he was dismissed after invoking the Fifth Amendment in an appearance before this committee last December. It is particularly significant that he declined to answer questions regarding his relationship with White. Information on Coe had been furnished to the White House as early as 25th February 1946, to the Attorney General on 23rd and 25th February 1946, and to the Treasury Department as early as 4th March 1946.

"From the foregoing, it is clear that the FBI called to the attention of the appropriate authorities the facts as alleged by reliable sources, which were substantial in pointing to a security risk, as they occurred."

(New York Herald Tribune, Paris, 19th November 1953)

The whole American press commented on the depositions of these three outstanding public personalities, and the New York Herald

Tribune weighed out the conclusions in a well-measured editorial, from which we have taken the following extracts:

"In two extraordinary presentations, watched by virtually the whole country, the principal actors in the White case have now had their say. Ex-President Truman's broadcast address was marked by a depth of bitterness and a violence of language rare in public life; he took the offensive in a broadside political attack on the Attorney General. Before a committee Mr. Brownell replied with a lawyer's cool skill. He got the discussion back to the question of blindness and laxity in the previous administration and stirred grave doubts on the ex-President's defence.

"Mr. Truman put the veracity of Mr. Brownell at the centre of the controversy; and now the public finds itself asking which of these two men is closer to the truth. Did Mr. Brownell lie when he said that Mr. Truman knowingly appointed a spy to the most important sensitive position he had ever held? Did Mr. Truman lie when he said that he deliberately let the appointment run its normal course in order to track down the spy ring? It is a degrading thing to ask such questions about public servants; actually 'lying' should not have to enter the discussion. Let it be admitted that Mr. Brownell overstated his case at Chicago. It will likewise have to be admitted even by his most partisan supporters that Mr. Truman clearly overstates now, in his efforts to put the best light possible on his past conduct, the degree to which he was influenced by a determined plan to track down the government spy ring.

"Certainly Mr. Brownell's testimony makes it appear that no concerted efforts were made by the democratic administration to remove those named by the FBI as part of the same spy ring with White. Long after White himself had left office, others (as the Attorney General made damningly plain) continued in positions of responsibility. No proof of any kind has been adduced by the ex-President to show that his plan for getting full evidence and taking firm action on suspected spies—assuming such a plan to have existed—was actually carried out. The Attorney General indeed stated specifically that he knew of no precautions or directives resulting from the decision to keep White in government employ. . . .

"Human motives are mixed . . . the vicious charge of untruth which Truman saw fit to level against the Attorney General need not be turned now against a former President of the United States. But what at this stage needs, in our opinion, to be turned against him is the charge of laxity and confusion in the highest and most serious of responsibilities. It is not pleasant to contemplate these matters which time has mercifully put behind us . . . but when men like Truman and those around him are shown to have been so blind and mistaken, the need to get at the facts is overpowering.

"Unfortunately, the facts are not simple . . . Mr. Truman would have preserved the country from infinite groping and uncertainty if he had appointed in his administration an impartial commission to sift all the evidence and state positive conclusions. He failed to do this; and in spite of a fighting defence, he cannot but be judged to have failed in convincing the country that he dealt effectively with the mortal threat of subversion."

(*New York Herald Tribune*, Paris, 19th November 1953)

IX

AMERICA AND ISRAEL

In the previous chapters of this work we have shown by reference to precise facts and documents—Zabrousky, Landman and Morgenthau—the enormous influence which American and principally Zionist Jews have exercised on the foreign policy of the USA government.

But quite recently an American diplomat called David Nes, who has retired after twenty-six years' service in the State Department, published an article in the London *Times* of 5th February 1971 which brought to light new information on this subject. Entitled "America's very special relationship with Israel", his article confirms and indeed amplifies everything that we have said and written in the present work. Reading this article, we receive the very distinct impression that American foreign policy is inspired, guided and virtually laid down by the Zionist lobby.

Mr. David Nes was well placed to know what he was talking about, for he was Chargé d'Affaires, representing the American government at Cairo, immediately before and after the Six Days War between Israel and the Arab States. The following passages contain the essence of the article in question, which was only published in the early editions of *The Times* of that date, and responsibility for which remains entirely with its author.

"The White House invitation and reception recently accorded Israel's Defence Minister, Moshe Dayan, is illustrative of the very special relationship the United States has developed with his country over the past twenty-two years. It is doubtful whether a NATO or SEATO defence chief would have been granted such high protocol treatment. Most would have had to be satisfied with meeting the Defence Secretary or, in exceptional cases, the Secretary of State or the Vice-President.

"When President Truman said in October 1948: 'We are pledged to a State of Israel, large enough, free enough and strong enough to make its people self-supporting and secure', the stage was set for the gradual establishment of an association between the United States and another country unique in American history. Today, that association is far closer in all areas—defence, economic collaboration, intelligence exchange, common citizenship, and mutual diplomatic support—than that enjoyed, for example, between the United States and Great Britain.

"Unique also is Israel's almost total immunity from criticism in the United States—a situation hardly paralleled by any of our European or Asian allies, many of whose faults and frailties are daily aired in our communications media and by our legislative representatives. Perhaps, as James Reston of the *New York Times* suggested a short while ago, '. . . you can put it down as a general rule that any criticism of Israel's policies will be attacked as anti-semitism'. And so it goes in reverse, with Israel's image as a small, democratic, courageous little country struggling to survive in a sea of uncivilized, bloodthirsty, pro-communist Arabs, representing, rightly or wrongly, the view of most Americans. A new, very impressive colour documentary film on *Israel and the Bible* sponsored by Billy Graham and to be shown in 1,200 churches throughout the United States each month, will support this image.

"In dollars and cents, America's assistance to Israel through the years, both governmental and private, has been prodigious. During the 20-year period between 1948–1968, the United States government economic aid totalled $11,000m, while dollar transfers from private sources amounted to $25,000m, a total of $36,000m, or $1,400 per capita on a current population of 2,500,000. This greatly exceeds on a per capita basis United States assistance to any ally and compares to $35 per capita to the peoples of thirteen neighbouring states. Since 1968, American assistance to Israel has greatly increased. Dollar transfers in 1970 reached $800m, and in 1971 will approximate $1.5 billion.

"Until 1967, we assured Israel a continuing supply of modern military equipment directed through West Germany and France and we were thus able to avoid Arab hostility. However, with the conclusion of German 'reparations' and De Gaulle's change in Middle East Policy, America has since 1967 become the exclusive purveyor of arms to Israel. Of greater significance is the fact that qualitatively America has provided aircraft, missiles, and electronic systems of greater sophistication and greater strike capability than those furnished to our NATO and SEATO allies. For example, Greece, Turkey and Iran, which form the northern tier defence line against the Soviet Union, have not yet received our Phantom aircraft. A few weeks ago, the House of Representatives passed an amendment to the Defence Procurement Bill giving the President open-ended authority to transfer military equipment to Israel without total cost limitation. . . . Great Britain at the height of its struggle against Hitler never received such a blank cheque. Nor, in more recent times, has South Vietnam. . . .

"In the area of nuclear weapons, the United States has also pursued an exceptional position vis-à-vis Israel. During the years when we were pressing over one hundred nations in the world community with whatever diplomatic, economic and military leverage we might have to adhere to the Nuclear Non-Proliferation Treaty, Israel alone was exempted from strong representations. In fact we may have encouraged Israel to refrain from assuming the obligations set forth in this international undertaking. Through a study prepared at White House request by the Rand Corporation of California, we provided Israel with the most advanced technical and political data on the effective use of nuclear weapons in the Middle East. The Jewish Press in December summarized the nuclear situation: 'The experts who before the Six Day War felt that India would become the next member of the nuclear club now believe that the next member will be Israel'. This in fact has already occurred . . . in contrast to our intense opposition to France's nuclear development, the United States has supported Israel in virtually an identical policy.

"In the exchange of intelligence, American co-operation with Israel is unprecedented and goes far beyond the special nuclear arrangements with Great Britain based on the McMahon Act. During the months before the June 1967 hostilities, the military intelligence requirements required by Washington from American Embassies, the Central Intelligence Agency and military intelligence staffs in the Middle East were very largely based on Israel's needs, not on American interests. The effectiveness of the Israeli air strikes on 5th June 1967 was assured at least in part by information on Egyptian airfields and aircraft disposition provided through American sources. With political and economic information, it has long been State Department practice to provide the Israeli Embassy in Washington with copies of all of our reports from Middle East Embassies considered to be of interest. A summary by Ray Vickers about this co-operation appeared in the Wall Street Journal on 12th February 1970. When the American Naval Intelligence ship Liberty was attacked by Israeli air and sea units in June 1967—with the loss of 34 dead and 71 injured—the incident resulted in minimum official reaction. It boggles the imagination to speculate as to the reaction were the attackers to have been British or French, much less Egyptian, as initially assumed.

"Israel also enjoys an exceptional position on the question of dual citizenship. Under long-standing citizenship laws an American voting in the elections or serving in the armed forces or government of a foreign country loses his citizenship. By a recent Supreme Court interpretation, Americans may serve in Israel in this manner without loss of citizenship. Under the Israeli Law of Return, an American Jew entering Israel is automatically given Israeli nationality.

"Since the war in June 1967, and particularly during the past year, American commitments to Israel have been greatly expanded. Before 1967 the United States was committed to Israel's territorial integrity within the 1948 armistice lines and to her economic viability. . . . In the United Nations Resolution of November 1967, America in effect opposed Israel's retention of the territories conquered by force the previous June. This fundamental position has now changed very radically. Last summer, in a series of statements from the Sam Clemente 'White House', the Nixon Administration would appear to have extended the territorial integrity commitment to include, until a final peace settlement, the occupied territories; to have moved from assuring a military balance, to guaranteeing Israel a 'military superiority capable of launching a rapid knock-out blow' against her neighbours, and to have supported Israel's continued 'racial exclusiveness', thereby negating our eighteen years of support for the United Nations Palestine refugee formula of 'repatriation or compensation'. When asked during the 10th December Press Conference whether America still adhered to its position on Israeli withdrawal from the 'occupied territories', President Nixon, for the first time, evaded the issue by saying that it was a matter for negotiation.

"Finally, the assignment and advancement of personnel in the Department of State to the top positions relating to the Middle East policy, have traditionally been subjected to prior approval by the American Zionist leadership. As an example in reverse, the firing of the United Nations Ambassador, Mr. Charles W. Yost, was demanded by the 'pro-Israeli lobby', as recently reported by the columnists Evans and Novak.

"This special relationship would appear to have the full and massive support of most Americans and certainly of the Congress and the press. It is hardly surprising therefore, that every Administration since that of President Truman has worked towards establishing closer and more cordial ties with Israel as one of the cardinal principles of American foreign policy. General Moshe Dayan, when he met President Nixon, was in a far more enviable position than other top foreign leaders visiting Washington, whether they be Mr. Heath, M. Pompidou, or Herr Willy Brandt, or representatives of Asian, African or Latin American countries friendly to the United States.

"Only history can provide the total explanation for this very special American-Israeli relationship. It has now reached a point where Israel's security and welfare is considered vital to American welfare, but our reaction to any threats against Israel is more intense than with any of our NATO or SEATO allies. One State Department humorist has said: 'Were Israel's survival to be seriously threatened, we would be in the Third World War in two minutes—with Berlin it might take several days! ' "

(*The Times*, 5th February 1971)

BIBLIOGRAPHY

M. BAR-ZOHAR, *Les Vengeurs*.

BARTZ, K., *Quand le ciel était en feu*.

BEATY, J., *The Iron Curtain over America*.

DILLON, DR. E. J., *The Peace Conference*.

DOENITZ, GRAND ADMIRAL, *Ten Years and Twenty Days*.

DOUSSINAGUE, J. M., *España tenia Razon*.

FLYNN, J. T., *While You Slept*.

The Forrestal Diaries.

GANNON, R. I., SJ, *The Cardinal Spellman Story*.

IRVING, D., *The Destruction of Dresden*.

KAUFMAN, T. N., *Germany Must Perish*.

LANDMAN, S., *Great Britain, the Jews and Palestine*.

LUDWIG, E., *A New Holy Alliance*.

MALYNSKI, E., *La Démocratie Victorieuse*.

MONTIGNY, J., *Le Complot contre la Paix*.

Morgenthau Diary

ROOSEVELT, E., *As He Saw It*.

SNOW, SIR C., *Science and Government*.

VEALE, F. J. P., *Advance to Barbarism*.

WHEELER-BENNETT, J. W., *The Drama of the German Army*.

WILLOUGHBY, MAJOR-GENERAL C. A., *Sorge, Soviet Master Spy*.

INDEX

www.ingramcontent.com/pod-product-compliance
Lightning Source LLC
Chambersburg PA
CBHW071350280326
41927CB00040B/2594